P9-API-304

Quick & Easy
Simple Chinese

p

Contents

Introduction 4

Chinese Pork & Potato Broth 6

Chicken, Noodle & Corn Soup 7

Mushroom Noodle Soup 8

Small Shrimp Rolls 9

Pork Dim Sum 10

Crispy Seaweed 11

Chinese Omelet 12

Son-in-Law Eggs 13

Asparagus Parcels 14

Oriental Salad 15

Noodle & Mango Salad 16

Shrimp Salad 17

Carrot & Cilantro Salad 18

Hot & Sour Duck Salad 19

Chinese Chicken Salad 20

Hot Rice Salad 21

Chicken & Paw-Paw Salad 22

Bean Sprout Salad 23

Hot & Sweet Salad 24

Paw-Paw Salad 25

Duck with Ginger & Lime 26

Lemon & Sesame Chicken 27

Cashew Chicken 28

Chicken Foo-Yong 29

Sweet & Sour Pork 30

Meatballs in Peanut Sauce 31

Beef & Beans 32

Soy & Sesame Beef 33

Lamb with Mushroom Sauce 34

Spicy Pork Balls 35

Crab with Chinese Cabbage 36

Small Shrimp Foo Yong 37

Seafood Omelet 38

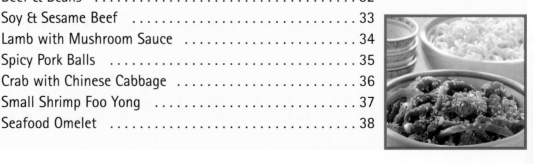

Trout with Pineapple 39
Fish with Ginger Butter 40
Seafood Medley 41
Shrimp with Vegetables 42
Fish with Black Bean Sauce 43
Mussels with Lemon Grass 44
Shrimp Stir-Fry 45
Mullet with Ginger 46
Shrimp & Sweetcorn Patties 47
Fried Squid Flowers 48
Scallop Pancakes 49
Sweet & Sour Cauliflower 50
Honey-Fried Chinese Cabbage 51
Spicy Eggplant 52
Lemon Chinese Cabbage 53
Broccoli & Black Bean Sauce 54
Caraway Cabbage 55
Deep-Fried Zucchini 56
Green & Black Bean Stir-Fry 57
Bamboo with Spinach 58
Vegetable Chop Suey 59
Bean Curd with Mushrooms 60
Bean Curd with Hot & Sweet Sauce 61
Bean Curd Casserole 62
Bean Curd with Bell Peppers 63
Egg Fried Rice 64
Chatuchak Fried Rice 65
Green Fried Rice 66
Vegetable Fried Rice 67
Chinese Risotto 68
Chicken Chow Mein 69
Cantonese Fried Noodles 70
Lamb with Noodles 71
Pork Chow Mein 72
Oyster Sauce Noodles 73
Noodles with Chili & Shrimp 74
Noodles with Shrimp 75
Chicken & Noodle One-Pot 76
Sweet Fruit Wontons 77
Exotic Fruit Salad 78
Lime Mousse with Mango 79

Introduction

The abundance of Chinese restaurants in the West demonstrates perfectly the popularity of Chinese cooking. Authentic dishes from all over China are assembled here for you to try at home. These recipes are delicious, incredibly easy to prepare and fortunately, for those with a busy lifestyle, many can be cooked in under an hour.

The Arrival of Chinese Cuisine

Chinese cuisine was introduced to the West when Chinese migrants settled in San Francisco during the Gold Rush. Since then, Chinese restaurants have spread throughout the world and Chinese ingredients and cooking equipment are now readily available.

Benefits of Eating Chinese

Chinese food is generally cooked rapidly over very high heat, using a minimum of oil, which preserves texture, flavor and nutrients. The ingredients include fish,

vegetables, and meats combined with noodles or rice, excellent sources of slow energy-releasing carbohydrates. High cholesterol ingredients, such as dairy products and red meats, are used sparingly, if at all. Chinese meals are well-balanced, not only in terms of a healthy diet, but also in their aim to provide complementary courses: spicy dishes are served with sweet-and-sour alternatives, dry-cooked dishes are accompanied by those in sauces.

Regional Cuisine

China is a vast country with an enormous variety of different climates which affect the agricultural productivity within each area. The harsh climate around the capital of Beijing in the North is very different to the milder coastal areas of the South; the influence of the Yangtse river is felt strongly at its delta near Shanghai in the East, while the West enjoys a mild humid climate and rich fertile soil in the shadow of the Tien Shan mountains. The regional cuisines are equally diverse.

The North. Dishes from the North are strongly flavored, using leeks, onions and garlic. Many dishes containing lamb, not pork, bear testimony to the Moslem culture introduced by invading Tartars from Central Asia. In northern areas wheat is used more frequently than rice, served as pancakes, noodles or dumplings.

The South. The first emigrant Chinese originated from Canton and its surrounding areas; this is still the most commonly known Chinese food in the West. Traditionally their foods, such as small fish, little parcels of meat or patties and dumplings are steam cooked. These include Dim Sum, which are served as snacks in teahouses.

The East. Benefiting enormously from the annual flooding of the Yangtze River, the East boasts very rich soil. The fertile plains allow growth of broccoli, sweet potatoes, pak choi, soya beans, tea, rice – the list is almost endless! Many of the traditional dishes are vegetarian and they vary enormously. Today, the regional cuisines of the east have been influenced by the city of Shanghai which has assimilated culinary influences from around the world. Dairy products have infiltrated Chinese kitchens, but duck, ham and fish in piquant spices still remain specialities.

The West. Benefiting from a mild climate, Szechuan is noted for its robust, richly colored spicy dishes. Szechuan cookery uses lots of garlic, ginger, onions, leeks and Szechuan peppercorns. Western China is renowned for its smoking, drying, pickling and salting techniques, used to preserve foods and enhance flavors.

Seven different ingredients are used to achieve seven very particular flavors in Szechuan cooking: sweet flavors use honey; salty ones, soy sauce; sour flavors, vinegar; bitter ones, onions or leeks; fragrant dishes, garlic or ginger; sesame flavors, sesame seed paste and hot recipes use chilies.

Ingredients

Chinese ingredients are widely available in supermarkets although it is worth investing in better quality versions of some of the oils, condiments and sauces from specialist shops.

Bamboo shoots. Bamboo shoots, although bland on their own, are used for their texture. To prepare fresh shoots, remove the tough outer skins and boil in water for 40–50 minutes.

Bean sauce. Available in cans or jars, this savory paste is black or yellow and made from crushed, salted soya beans, flour and four spices. Red paste is used for sweet sauces.

Chilies. Fiery hot chili oil contains chili flakes and should be used with caution. Chili bean sauce contains soya beans and uses the chilies for flavor – it should

also be used sparingly. If using fresh chilies remember that small pointed chilies are usually significantly hotter than larger, more rounded alternatives. The seeds are the hottest part so removing these will reduce the potency of the peppers.

Chinese five-spice. The five spices are: star anise, fennel seeds, cinnamon, cloves and Szechuan pepper. They produce a musty, pungent aroma and add a delicious and distinctive Chinese flavor to dishes when added sparingly.

Chinese rice wine and vinegar. Rice wine is made from glutinous rice and resembles dry sherry (which can be used as a suitable cooking alternative). Rice vinegar is distilled from Chinese rice wine and is stronger than red

vinegar. Cider or white wine vinegars can be used instead.

Dried mushrooms. Shiitake mushrooms have a strong flavor; they are expensive but a little goes a long way. The dried mushrooms need to be soaked for 20–30 minutes before use; the water can be kept for stock.

Ginger. Ginger root can be bought in the supermarket, look for plump pieces with shiny unblemished skin. Cut the amount you need, peel it then chop, slice or grate it. Fresh ginger will keep for weeks in a cool, dry place. Ground ginger is not a good substitute.

Hoisin sauce. Made from soya beans, sugar, flour, vinegar, chilies, garlic, sesame oil and salt. It is used for flavoring in small quantities combined with soy sauce or used alone on duck, spare ribs or seafood.

Lemon grass. The lower part of lemon grass stems add a slightly citrus flavor to a dish. It should be removed before serving if used whole.

Star anise. This is a star-shaped fruit with a strong aniseed flavor. Usually used ground, pods can be used although they should be removed before serving.

Cooking equipment

A good quality wok is essential if you want to achieve an authentic Chinese taste. Traditionally made from cast iron, there are now many different types: stainless steel woks are not recommended as they scorch, and some non-stick woks cannot tolerate the very high temperatures required. Food should be tossed or stirred continuously to cook evenly.

There are few special accessories required for Chinese cooking. A lid for your wok is essential for steaming. Cleavers are used to chop, dice and cut everything from shellfish and herbs, to meat and vegetables. Chop sticks are used for preparation – they are unlikely to damage delicate food – as well as for eating.

KEY		
	Simplicity level 1 – 3 (1 easiest, 3 slightly harder)	
	Preparation time	
	Cooking time	

Chinese Potato & Pork Broth

In this recipe the pork is seasoned with traditional Chinese flavorings – soy sauce, rice wine vinegar and a dash of sesame oil.

NUTRITIONAL INFORMATION

Calories 166	Sugars 2g
Protein 10g	Fat 5g
Carbohydrate ...26g	Saturates 1g

5 MINS   20 MINS

SERVES 4

I N G R E D I E N T S

4½ cups chicken stock

2 large potatoes, diced

2 tbsp rice wine vinegar

2 tbsp cornstarch

4 tbsp water

4½ oz pork fillet, sliced

1 tbsp light soy sauce

1 tsp sesame oil

1 carrot, cut into very thin strips

1 tsp ginger root, chopped

3 scallions,
  sliced thinly

1 bell pepper, sliced

8 oz can bamboo shoots,
  drained

VARIATION

For extra heat,
add 1 chopped red chili
or 1 tsp of chili powder
to the soup in step 5.

1 Add the chicken stock, diced potatoes and 1 tbsp of the rice wine vinegar to a saucepan and bring to the boil. Reduce the heat until the stock is just simmering.

2 Mix the cornstarch with the water then stir into the hot stock.

3 Bring the stock back to the boil, stirring until thickened, then reduce the heat until it is just simmering again.

4 Place the pork slices in a dish and season with the remaining rice wine vinegar, the soy sauce and sesame oil.

5 Add the pork slices, carrot strips and ginger to the stock and cook for 10 minutes. Stir in the scallions, red bell pepper and bamboo shoots. Cook for a further 5 minutes. Pour the soup into warmed bowls and serve immediately.

Chicken, Noodle & Corn Soup

The vermicelli gives this Chinese-style soup an Italian twist, but you can use egg noodles if you prefer.

NUTRITIONAL INFORMATION

Calories . . . . .401 Sugars 6g
Protein . . . . .31g Fat 24g
Carbohydrate . . .17g Saturates 13g

5 MINS   25 MINS

SERVES 4

INGREDIENTS

1 lb boned chicken breasts,
    cut into strips

5 cups chicken stock

⅝ cup heavy cream

¾ cup dried vermicelli

1 tbsp cornstarch

3 tbsp milk

6 oz corn kernels

salt and pepper

finely chopped scallions,
    to garnish (optional)

1 Put the chicken strips, chicken stock and heavy cream into a large saucepan and bring to the boil over a low heat.

2 Reduce the heat slightly and simmer for about 20 minutes. Season the soup with salt and black pepper to taste.

3 Meanwhile, cook the vermicelli in lightly salted boiling water for 10-12 minutes, until just tender. Drain the pasta and keep warm.

4 In a small bowl, mix together the cornstarch and milk to make a smooth paste. Stir the cornstarch paste into the soup until thickened.

5 Add the corn and vermicelli to the pan and heat through.

6 Transfer the soup to a warm tureen or individual soup bowls, garnish with scallions, if desired, and serve immediately.

VARIATION

For crab and sweetcorn soup, substitute 1 lb cooked crabmeat for the chicken breasts. Flake the crabmeat well before adding it to the saucepan and reduce the cooking time by 10 minutes.

Mushroom Noodle Soup

A light, refreshing clear soup of mushrooms, cucumber and small pieces of rice noodles, flavored with soy sauce and a touch of garlic.

NUTRITIONAL INFORMATION

Calories 84	Sugars 1g	
Protein 1g	Fat 8g	
Carbohydrate 3g	Saturates 1g	

🍲 5 MINS   🕐 10 MINS

SERVES 4

I N G R E D I E N T S

4½ oz flat or open-cup
   mushrooms

½ cucumber

2 scallions

1 garlic clove

2 tbsp vegetable oil

¼ cup Chinese rice
   noodles

¾ tsp salt

1 tbsp soy sauce

1 Wash the mushrooms and pat dry on paper towels. Slice thinly. Do not remove the peel as this adds more flavor.

2 Halve the cucumber lengthways. Scoop out the seeds, using a teaspoon, and slice the cucumber thinly.

3 Chop the scallions finely and cut the garlic clove into thin strips.

4 Heat the vegetable oil in a large saucepan or wok.

5 Add the scallions and garlic to the pan or wok and stir-fry for 30 seconds. Add the mushrooms and stir-fry for 2–3 minutes.

6 Stir in 2½ cups water. Break the noodles into short lengths and add to the soup. Bring to the boil, stirring occasionally.

7 Add the cucumber slices, salt and soy sauce, and simmer for 2–3 minutes.

8 Serve the mushroom noodle soup in warmed bowls, distributing the noodles and vegetables evenly.

COOK'S TIP

Scooping the seeds out from the cucumber gives it a prettier effect when sliced, and also helps to reduce any bitterness, but if you prefer, you can leave them in.

Small Shrimp Rolls

This variation of a spring roll is made with shrimps, stir-fried with shallots, carrot, cucumber, bamboo shoots and rice.

NUTRITIONAL INFORMATION

Calories 388   Sugars 2g
Protein . . . . .9g   Fat 25g
Carbohydrate . . .33g   Saturates 6g

10 MINS   15 MINS

SERVES 4

I N G R E D I E N T S

2 tbsp vegetable oil

3 shallots, chopped very finely

1 carrot, cut into matchstick pieces

3 inch piece of cucumber, cut into matchstick pieces

½ cup bamboo shoots, shredded finely

½ cup peeled small shrimp

½ cup cooked long-grain rice

1 tbsp fish sauce or light soy sauce

1 tsp sugar

2 tsp cornstarch, blended in 2 tbsp cold water

10 inch spring roll wrappers

oil for deep-frying

salt and pepper

plum sauce, to serve

T O   G A R N I S H

scallion brushes

sprigs of fresh cilantro

1 Heat the oil in a wok and add the shallots, carrot, cucumber and bamboo shoots. Stir-fry briskly for 2–3 minutes. Add the shrimp and cooked rice, and cook for a further 2 minutes. Season.

2 Mix together the fish sauce or soy sauce, sugar and blended cornstarch. Add to the stir-fry and cook, stirring constantly, for about 1 minute, until thickened. Leave to cool slightly.

3 Place spoonfuls of the shrimp and vegetable mixture on the spring roll wrappers. Dampen the edges and roll them up to enclose the filling completely.

4 Heat the oil for deep-frying and fry the spring rolls until crisp and golden brown. Drain on paper towels. Serve the rolls garnished with scallion brushes and fresh cilantro and accompanied by the plum sauce.

Pork Dim Sum

These small steamed parcels are traditionally served as an appetizer and are very adaptable to your favorite fillings.

NUTRITIONAL INFORMATION

Calories 478   Sugars 3g
Protein ....33g   Fat 29g
Carbohydrate ...21g   Saturates 9g

 10 MINS   15 MINS

SERVES 4

I N G R E D I E N T S

14 oz ground pork

2 scallions, chopped

1¾ oz canned bamboo shoots, drained, rinsed and chopped

1 tbsp light soy sauce

1 tbsp dry sherry

2 tsp sesame oil

2 tsp superfine sugar

1 egg white, lightly beaten

4½ tsp cornstarch

24 wonton wrappers

1 Place the ground pork, scallions, bamboo shoots, soy sauce, dry sherry, sesame oil, superfine sugar and beaten egg white in a large mixing bowl and mix until all the ingredients are thoroughly combined.

2 Stir in the cornstarch, mixing until thoroughly incorporated with the other ingredients.

3 Spread out the wonton wrappers on a counter. Place a spoonful of the pork and vegetable mixture in the centre of each wonton wrapper and lightly brush the edges of the wrappers with water.

4 Bring the sides of the wrappers together in the centre of the filling, pinching firmly together.

5 Line a steamer with a clean, damp dish cloth and arrange the wontons inside.

6 Cover and steam for 5–7 minutes, until the dim sum are cooked through. Serve immediately.

COOK'S TIP

Bamboo steamers are designed to rest on the sloping sides of a wok above the water. They are available in a range of sizes.

Crispy Seaweed

This tasty Chinese starter is not all it seems – the 'seaweed' is in fact bok choy which is fried, salted and tossed with pine nuts.

NUTRITIONAL INFORMATION

Calories	214	Sugars	........14g
Protein	.........6g	Fat	..........15g
Carbohydrate	...15g	Saturates	.......2g

 10 MINS   5 MINS

SERVES 4

INGREDIENTS

2 lb 4 oz bok choy

peanut oil, for deep-frying (about 3¾ cups)

1 tsp salt

1 tbsp superfine sugar

2½ tbsp toasted pine nuts

1   Rinse the bok choy leaves under cold running water and then pat dry thoroughly with absorbent paper towels.

2   Discarding any tough outer leaves, roll each pak choi leaf up, then slice through thinly so that the leaves are finely shredded. Alternatively, use a food processor to shred the bok choy.

COOK'S TIP

The tough, outer leaves of bok choy are discarded as these will spoil the overall taste and texture of the dish.

Use savoy cabbage instead of the bok choy if it is unavailable, drying the leaves thoroughly before frying.

3   Heat the peanut oil in a large wok or heavy-based skillet.

4   Carefully add the shredded bok choy leaves to the wok or skillet and fry for about 30 seconds or until they shrivel up and become crispy (you will probably need to do this in several batches, depending on the size of the wok).

5   Remove the crispy seaweed from the wok with a slotted spoon and drain on absorbent paper towels.

6   Transfer the crispy seaweed to a large bowl and toss with the salt, sugar and pine nuts. Serve immediately.

Chinese Omelet

This is a fairly filling omelet, as it contains chicken and shrimp. It is cooked as a whole omelet and then sliced for serving.

NUTRITIONAL INFORMATION

Calories	309	Sugars	.........0g
Protein	........34g	Fat	..........19g
Carbohydrate	...0.2g	Saturates	.......5g

5 MINS   5 MINS

SERVES 4

INGREDIENTS

8 eggs

2 cups cooked chicken, shredded

12 jumbo shrimp,
    peeled and deveined

2 tbsp chopped chives

2 tsp light soy sauce

dash of chili sauce

2 tbsp vegetable oil

1 Lightly beat the eggs in a large mixing bowl.

2 Add the shredded chicken and jumbo shrimp to the eggs, mixing well.

3 Stir in the chopped chives, light soy sauce and chili sauce, mixing well to combine all the ingredients.

4 Heat the vegetable oil in a large preheated skillet over a medium heat.

5 Add the egg mixture to the skillet, tilting the pan to coat the base completely.

6 Cook over a medium heat, gently stirring the omelet with a fork, until the surface is just set and the underside is a golden brown color.

7 When the omelet is set, slide it out of the pan, with the aid of a spatula.

8 Cut the Chinese omelet into squares or slices and serve immediately. Alternatively, serve the omelet as a main course for two people.

VARIATION

You could add extra flavor to the omelet by stirring in 3 tablespoons of finely chopped fresh cilantro or 1 teaspoon of sesame seeds with the chives in step 3.

Son-in-Law Eggs

This recipe is supposedly so called because it is an easy dish for a son-in-law to cook to impress his new mother-in-law!

NUTRITIONAL INFORMATION

Calories	229	Sugars	.........8g
Protein	.........9g	Fat	..........18g
Carbohydrate	....8g	Saturates	.......3g

15 MINS   15 MINS

SERVES 4

INGREDIENTS

6 eggs, hard cooked and shelled

4 tbsp. sunflower oil

1 onion, sliced thinly

2 fresh red chilies, sliced

2 tbsp sugar

1 tbsp water

2 tsp tamarind pulp

1 tbsp liquid seasoning, such
   as Maggi

rice, to serve

1 Prick the hard-cooked eggs 2 or 3 times with a toothpick.

2 Heat the sunflower oil in a wok and fry the eggs until crispy and golden. Drain on absorbent paper towels.

3 Halve the eggs lengthways and put on a serving dish.

4 Reserve one tablespoon of the oil, pour off the rest, then heat the tablespoonful in the wok. Cook the onion and chilies over a high heat until golden and slightly crisp. Drain on paper towels.

5 Heat the sugar, water, tamarind pulp and liquid seasoning in the wok and simmer for 5 minutes until thickened.

6 Pour the sauce over the eggs and spoon over the onion and chilies. Serve immediately with rice.

COOK'S TIP

Tamarind pulp is sold in oriental stores, and is quite sour. If it is not available, use twice the amount of lemon juice in its place.

Aspagarus Parcels

These small parcels are ideal as part of a main meal and irresistible as a quick snack with extra plum sauce for dipping.

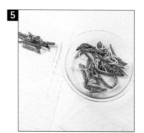

NUTRITIONAL INFORMATION

Calories	194	Sugars	.........2g
Protein	.........3g	Fat	..........16g
Carbohydrate	....11g	Saturates	.......4g

 5 MINS   25 MINS

SERVES 4

I N G R E D I E N T S

3½ oz fine tip asparagus

1 red bell pepper, deseeded and thinly sliced

½ cup bean sprouts

2 tbsp plum sauce

1 egg yolk

8 sheets filo pastry

oil, for deep-frying

1 Place the asparagus, bell pepper and beansprouts in a large mixing bowl.

2 Add the plum sauce to the vegetables and mix until well combined.

3 Beat the egg yolk and set aside until required.

4 Lay the sheets of filo pastry out on to a clean counter.

5 Place a little of the asparagus and red bell pepper filling at the top end of each filo pastry sheet. Brush the edges of the filo pastry with a little of the beaten egg yolk.

6 Roll up the filo pastry, tucking in the ends and enclosing the filling like a spring roll. Repeat with the remaining filo sheets.

7 Heat the oil for deep-frying in a large preheated wok. Carefully cook the parcels, 2 at a time, in the hot oil for 4–5 minutes or until crispy.

8 Remove the parcels with a slotted spoon and leave to drain on absorbent paper towels.

9 Transfer the parcels to warm serving plates and serve immediately.

COOK'S TIP

Be sure to use fine-tipped asparagus as it is more tender than the larger stems.

Oriental Salad

This colorful crisp salad has a fresh orange dressing and is topped with crunchy vermicelli.

NUTRITIONAL INFORMATION

Calories	...139	Sugars	...8g
Protein	...5g	Fat	...7g
Carbohydrate	...15g	Saturates	...1g

🔔 🔔

 10 MINS   5 MINS

SERVES 4

I N G R E D I E N T S

¼ cup dried vermicelli

½ head Chinese cabbage

2 cups bean sprouts

6 radishes

4½ oz snow peas

1 large carrot

4½ oz sprouting beans

D R E S S I N G

juice of 1 orange

1 tbsp sesame seeds, toasted

1 tsp honey

1 tsp sesame oil

1 tbsp hazelnut oil

1 Break the vermicelli into small strands. Heat a wok and dry-fry the vermicelli until lightly golden.

COOK'S TIP

Make your own sprouting beans by soaking mung and aduki beans overnight in cold water, drain and rinse. Place in a large jar covered with muslin to secure it. Lay the jar on its side and place in indirect light. For the next 3 days rinse the beans once each day in cold water until they are ready to eat.

2 Remove from the pan with a slotted spoon and set aside until required.

3 Using a sharp knife or food processor, shred the Chinese cabbage and wash with the bean sprouts. Drain thoroughly and place the leaves and bean sprouts in a large mixing bowl.

4 Thinly slice the radishes. Trim the snow peas and cut each into 3 pieces.

Cut the carrot into thin matchsticks. Add the sprouting beans and prepared vegetables to the bowl.

5 Place all the dressing ingredients in a screw-top jar and shake until well-blended. Pour over the salad and toss.

6 Transfer the salad to a serving bowl and sprinkle over the reserved vermicelli before serving.

Noodle & Mango Salad

Fruit combines well with the peanut dressing, bell peppers and chili in this delicous hot salad.

NUTRITIONAL INFORMATION

Calories	368	Sugars	........11g
Protein	........11g	Fat	..........26g
Carbohydrate	...24g	Saturates	.......5g

 15 MINS   5 MINS

SERVES 4

INGREDIENTS

9 oz thread egg noodles

2 tbsp peanut oil

4 shallots, sliced

2 cloves garlic, crushed

1 red chili, deseeded and sliced

1 red bell pepper, deseeded and sliced

1 green bell pepper, deseeded and sliced

1 ripe mango, sliced into thin strips

¼ cup salted peanuts, chopped

DRESSING

4 tbsp peanut butter

⅓ cup coconut milk

1 tbsp tomato paste

1 Place the egg noodles in a large dish or bowl. Pour over enough boiling water to cover the noodles and leave to stand for 10 minutes.

COOK'S TIP

If preferred, gently heat the peanut dressing before pouring over the noodle salad.

2 Heat the peanut oil in a large preheated wok or skillet.

3 Add the shallots, crushed garlic, chili and bell pepper slices to the wok or skillet and stir-fry for 2–3 minutes.

4 Drain the egg noodles thoroughly in a colander. Add the drained noodles and mango slices to the wok or skillet and heat through for about 2 minutes.

5 Transfer the noodle and mango salad to warmed serving dishes and scatter with chopped peanuts.

6 To make the dressing, mix together the peanut butter, coconut milk and tomato paste then spoon over the noodle salad. Serve immediately.

Shrimp Salad

Noodles and bean sprouts form the basis of this refreshing salad which combines the flavors of fruit and shrimp.

NUTRITIONAL INFORMATION

Calories 359	Sugars 4g
Protein 31g	Fat 15g
Carbohydrate . . .25g	Saturates 2g

 15 MINS   🕐 5 MINS

SERVES 4

I N G R E D I E N T S

9 oz fine egg noodles

3 tbsp sunflower oil

1 tbsp sesame oil

1 tbsp sesame seeds

1½ cups bean sprouts

1 ripe mango, sliced

6 scallions, sliced

2¾ oz radish, sliced

350 g/12 oz peeled cooked shrimp

2 tbsp light soy sauce

1 tbsp sherry

1 Place the egg noodles in a large bowl and pour over enough boiling water to cover. Leave to stand for 10 minutes.

2 Drain the noodles thoroughly and pat dry with paper towels.

COOK'S TIP

If fresh mango is unavailable, use canned mango slices, rinsed and drained, instead.

3 Heat the sunflower oil in a large wok or skillet and stir-fry the noodles for 5 minutes, tossing frequently.

4 Remove the wok from the heat and add the sesame oil, sesame seeds and bean sprouts, tossing to mix well.

5 In a separate bowl, mix together the sliced mango, scallions, radish and shrimp. Stir in the light soy sauce and sherry and mix until thoroughly combined.

6 Toss the shrimp mixture with the noodles and transfer to a serving dish. Alternatively, arrange the noodles around the edge of a serving plate and pile the shrimp mixture into the centre. Serve immediately as this salad is best eaten warm.

Carrot & Cilantro Salad

This tangy, crunchy salad makes an ideal accompaniment to many Chinese main courses.

NUTRITIONAL INFORMATION

Calories	50	Sugars	.........4g
Protein	.........1g	Fat	..........3g
Carbohydrate	....5g	Saturates	.....0.4g

5 MINS   0 MINS

SERVES 4

INGREDIENTS

4 large carrots

2 celery stalks, cut into matchsticks

2 tbsp roughly chopped fresh cilantro

DRESSING

1 tbsp sesame oil

1½ tbsp rice vinegar

½ tsp sugar

½ tsp salt

1 To create flower-shaped carrot slices, as shown, cut several grooves lengthways along each carrot before slicing it.

2 Slice each carrot into very thin slices, using the slicing cutter of a grater.

3 Combine the carrot, celery and cilantro in a bowl.

4 To make the dressing, combine the sesame oil, rice vinegar, sugar and salt in a bowl.

5 Just before serving, toss the carrot, celery and cilantro mixture in the dressing and transfer to a serving dish.

Hot & Sour Duck Salad

This is a lovely tangy salad, drizzled with a lime juice and fish sauce dressing. It makes a splendid starter or light main course dish.

NUTRITIONAL INFORMATION

Calories 236	Sugars 3g
Protein 27g	Fat 10g
Carbohydrate ...10g	Saturates 3g

🥗 40 MINS   🕐 5 MINS

SERVES 4

INGREDIENTS

2 heads crisp salad lettuce, washed and separated into leaves

2 shallots, thinly sliced

4 scallions, chopped

1 celery stalk, finely sliced into julienne strips

2 inch piece cucumber, cut into julienne strips

4½ oz bean sprouts

7 oz can water chestnuts, drained and sliced

4 duck breast fillets, roasted and sliced

orange slices, to serve

DRESSING

3 tbsp fish sauce

1½ tbsp lime juice

2 garlic cloves, crushed

1 red chili pepper, seeded and very finely chopped

1 green chili pepper, seeded and very finely chopped

1 tsp palm or brown crystal sugar

1 Place the lettuce leaves into a large mixing bowl. Add the sliced shallots, chopped scallions, celery strips, cucumber strips, bean sprouts and sliced water chestnuts. Toss well to mix. Place the mixture on a large serving platter.

2 Arrange the duck breast slices on top of the salad in an attractive overlapping pattern.

3 To make the dressing, put the fish sauce, lime juice, garlic, chilies and sugar into a small saucepan. Heat gently, stirring constantly. Taste and adjust the piquancy if liked by adding more lime juice, or add more fish sauce to reduce the sharpness.

4 Drizzle the warm salad dressing over the duck salad and serve immediately with orange slices.

Chinese Chicken Salad

This is a refreshing dish suitable for a summer meal or light lunch.

NUTRITIONAL INFORMATION

Calories 162	Sugars 3g
Protein 15g	Fat 10g
Carbohydrate 5g	Saturates 2g

25 MINS | 10 MINS

SERVES 4

INGREDIENTS

8 oz skinless, boneless chicken breasts

2 tsp light soy sauce

1 tsp sesame oil

1 tsp sesame seeds

2 tbsp vegetable oil

4½ oz bean sprouts

1 red bell pepper, seeded and thinly sliced

1 carrot, cut into matchsticks

3 baby corn cobs, sliced

snipped chives and carrot matchsticks, to garnish

SAUCE

2 tsp rice wine vinegar

1 tbsp light soy sauce

dash of chili oil

1 Place the chicken breasts in a shallow glass dish.

2 Mix together the soy sauce and sesame oil and pour over the chicken. Sprinkle with the sesame seeds and let stand for 20 minutes, turning the chicken over occasionally.

3 Remove the chicken from the marinade and cut the meat into thin slices.

4 Heat the vegetable oil in a preheated wok or large skillet. Add the chicken and fry for 4-5 minutes, until cooked through and golden brown on both sides. Remove the chicken from the wok with a slotted spoon, set aside and leave to cool.

5 Add the bean sprouts, bell pepper, carrot and baby corn cobs to the wok and stir-fry for 2-3 minutes. Remove from the wok with a slotted spoon, set aside and leave to cool.

6 To make the sauce, mix together the rice wine vinegar, light soy sauce and chili oil.

7 Arrange the chicken and vegetables together on a serving plate. Spoon the sauce over the salad, garnish with chives and carrot matchsticks and serve.

Hot Rice Salad

Nutty brown rice combines well with peanuts and a sweet and sour mixture of fruit and vegetables in this tangy combination.

NUTRITIONAL INFORMATION

Calories 464	Sugars 17g	
Protein 15g	Fat 24g	
Carbohydrate ...52g	Saturates 4g	

5 MINS   30 MINS

SERVES 4

I N G R E D I E N T S

1½ cups brown rice

1 bunch scallions

1 red bell pepper

4½ oz radishes

15 oz can pineapple pieces in natural juice, drained

2 cups bean sprouts

¾ cup dry-roasted peanuts

D R E S S I N G

2 tbsp crunchy peanut butter

1 tbsp peanut oil

2 tbsp light soy sauce

2 tbsp white wine vinegar

2 tsp clear honey

1 tsp chili powder

½ tsp garlic salt

pepper

3 To make the dressing, place the crunchy peanut butter, peanut oil, light soy sauce, white wine vinegar, honey, chili powder, garlic salt and pepper in a small bowl and whisk for a few seconds until well combined.

4 Drain the rice thoroughly and place in a heatproof bowl.

1 Put the rice in a pan and cover with water. Bring to the boil, then cover and simmer for 30 minutes until tender.

2 Meanwhile, chop the scallions, using a sharp knife. Deseed and chop the red bell pepper and thinly slice the radishes.

5 Heat the dressing in a small saucepan for 1 minute and then toss into the rice and mix well.

6 Working quickly, stir the pineapple pieces, scallions, bell pepper, bean sprouts and peanuts into the mixture in the bowl.

7 Pile the hot rice salad into a warmed serving dish.

8 Arrange the radish slices around the outside of the salad and serve immediately.

Chicken & Paw-Paw Salad

Try this recipe with a selection of different fruits for an equally tasty salad.

NUTRITIONAL INFORMATION

Calories	408	Sugars	.........8g
Protein	........30g	Fat	..........28g
Carbohydrate	...10g	Saturates	.......5g

5 MINS   15 MINS

SERVES 4

INGREDIENTS

4 skinless, boneless chicken
   breasts

1 red chili, deseeded and chopped

1⅔ tbsp red wine
   vinegar

⅓ cup olive oil

1 paw-paw, peeled

1 avocado, peeled

4½ oz alfalfa sprouts

4½ oz bean sprouts

salt and pepper

TO GARNISH

diced red bell pepper

diced cucumber

1 Poach the chicken breasts in boiling water for about 15 minutes or until cooked through.

2 Remove the chicken with a slotted spoon and set aside to cool.

3 To make the dressing, combine the chili, red wine vinegar and olive oil, season well with salt and pepper and set aside.

4 Place the chicken breasts on a chopping board. Using a very sharp knife, cut the chicken breasts across the grain into thin diagonal slices. Set aside.

5 Slice the paw-paw and avocado to the same thickness as the chicken.

6 Arrange the slices of paw-paw and avocado, together with the chicken, in an alternating pattern on four serving plates.

7 Arrange the alfalfa sprouts and bean sprouts on the serving plates and garnish with the diced red bell pepper and cucumber. Serve the salad with the dressing.

VARIATION

Try this recipe with peaches or nectarines instead of paw-paw.

Bean Sprout Salad

This is a very light dish and is ideal on its own for a summer meal or as a starter.

NUTRITIONAL INFORMATION

Calories 70   Sugars 5g
Protein . . . . .4g   Fat 3g
Carbohydrate . . . .7g   Saturates 0.5g

10 MINS   5 MINS

SERVES 4

INGREDIENTS

1 green bell pepper, seeded

1 carrot

1 celery stalk

2 tomatoes, finely chopped

12 oz bean sprouts

1 small cucumber

1 garlic clove, crushed

dash of chili sauce

2 tbsp light soy sauce

1 tsp wine vinegar

2 tsp sesame oil

16 fresh chives

1 Using a sharp knife, cut the green bell pepper, carrot and celery into matchsticks and finely chop the tomatoes.

2 Blanch the bean sprouts in boiling water for 1 minute. Drain well and rinse under cold water. Drain thoroughly again.

3 Cut the cucumber in half lengthways. Scoop out the seeds with a teaspoon and discard. Cut the flesh into matchsticks.

4 Mix the cucumber with the bean sprouts, green bell pepper, carrot, tomatoes and celery.

5 To make the dressing, mix together the garlic, chili sauce, soy sauce, wine vinegar and sesame oil in a small bowl.

6 Pour the dressing over the vegetables, tossing well to coat.

7 Spoon the bean sprout salad into a serving dish or on to 4 individual serving plates. Garnish the salad with fresh chives and serve.

VARIATION

Substitute 12 oz cooked, cooled green beans or snow peas for the cucumber. Vary the bean sprouts for a different flavor. Try adzuki bean or alfalfa sprouts, as well as the better-known mung and soya bean sprouts.

Hot & Sweet Salad

This salad is made by mixing fruit and vegetables with the sharp, sweet and fishy flavors of the dressing.

NUTRITIONAL INFORMATION

Calories	169	Sugars 8g
Protein	. . . . .14g	Fat 8g
Carbohydrate	. . . .11g	Saturates 1g

 15 MINS   0 MINS

SERVES 4

I N G R E D I E N T S

9 oz white cabbage, finely shredded

2 tomatoes, skinned, seeded and chopped

9 oz cooked green beans, halved if large

4½ oz peeled shrimp

1 paw-paw, peeled, seeded and chopped

1-2 fresh red chilies, seeded and very finely sliced

scant ⅓ cup roasted salted peanuts, crushed

handful of lettuce or baby spinach leaves, shredded or torn into small pieces

D R E S S I N G

4 tbsp lime juice

2 tbsp fish sauce

sugar, to taste

pepper

1 Mix the white cabbage with the tomatoes, green beans, shrimp, three-quarters of the paw-paw and half of the chilies in a large mixing bowl.

2 Stir in two-thirds of the crushed peanuts and mix well.

3 Line the rim of a large serving plate with the lettuce or spinach leaves and pile the salad mixture into the centre of the leaves.

4 To make the dressing, beat the lime juice with the fish sauce and add sugar and pepper to taste. Drizzle over the salad.

5 Scatter the top with the remaining paw-paw, chilies and crushed peanuts. Serve at once.

COOK'S TIP

To skin tomatoes, make a cross at the base with a very sharp knife, then immerse in a bowl of boiling water for a few minutes. Remove with a slotted spoon and peel off the skin.

Paw-Paw Salad

Choose firm paw-paws for this delicious salad.

NUTRITIONAL INFORMATION

Calories	193	Sugars	........11g
Protein	.........3g	Fat	..........15g
Carbohydrate	...12g	Saturates	.......2g

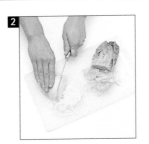

 10 MINS   0 MINS

SERVES 4

INGREDIENTS

DRESSING

4 tbsp olive oil

1 tbsp fish sauce or light soy sauce

2 tbsp lime or lemon juice

1 tbsp dark muscovado sugar

1 tsp finely chopped fresh red or
green chili

SALAD

1 crisp lettuce

¼ small white cabbage

2 paw-paws

2 tomatoes

¼ cup roasted peanuts,
chopped roughly

4 scallions, trimmed
and sliced thinly

basil leaves, to garnish

1 To make the dressing, whisk together the oil, fish sauce or soy sauce, lime or lemon juice, sugar and chili. Set aside, stirring occasionally to dissolve the sugar.

2 Shred the lettuce and white cabbage, then toss together and arrange on a large serving plate.

3 Peel the paw-paws and slice them in half. Scoop out the seeds, then slice the flesh thinly. Arrange on top of the lettuce and cabbage.

4 Soak the tomatoes in a bowl of boiling water for 1 minute, then lift out and peel. Remove the seeds and chop the flesh. Arrange on the salad greens.

5 Scatter the peanuts and scallions over the top. Whisk the dressing and pour over the salad. Garnish with basil leaves and serve at once.

COOK'S TIP

Choose plain, unsalted peanuts and toast them under the broiler until golden to get the best flavor. Take care not to burn them, as they brown very quickly.

Duck with Ginger & Lime

Just the thing for a lazy summer day – roasted duck sliced and served with a dressing made of ginger, lime juice, sesame oil and fish sauce.

NUTRITIONAL INFORMATION

Calories	529	Sugars	.........3g
Protein	........38g	Fat	..........41g
Carbohydrate	....3g	Saturates	.......6g

20 MINS · 25 MINS

SERVES 4

INGREDIENTS

3 boneless Barbary duck breasts, about 9 oz each

salt

DRESSING

½ cup olive oil

2 tsp sesame oil

2 tbsp lime juice

grated rind and juice of 1 orange

2 tsp fish sauce

1 tbsp grated fresh ginger

1 garlic clove, crushed

2 tsp light soy sauce

3 scallions, finely chopped

1 tsp sugar

about 9 oz assorted greens

orange slices, to garnish (optional)

1 Wash the duck breasts, dry on paper towels, then cut in half. Prick the skin all over with a fork and season well with salt. Place the duck pieces, skin-side down, on a wire rack or trivet over a roasting pan.

2 Cook the duck in a preheated oven for 10 minutes, then turn over and cook for a further 12–15 minutes, or until the duck is cooked, but still pink in the centre, and the skin is crisp.

3 To make the dressing, beat the olive oil and sesame oil with the lime juice, orange rind and juice, fish sauce, grated fresh ginger , garlic, light soy sauce, scallions and sugar until well blended.

4 Remove the duck from the oven, and allow to cool. Using a sharp knife, cut the duck into thick slices.

5 Add a little of the dressing to moisten and coat the duck.

6 To serve, arrange assorted salad greens on a serving dish. Top with the sliced duck breasts and drizzle with the remaining salad dressing.

7 Garnish with orange slices, if using, then serve at once.

Lemon & Sesame Chicken

Sesame seeds have a strong flavor which adds nuttiness to recipes. They are perfect for coating these thin chicken strips.

NUTRITIONAL INFORMATION

Calories 273	Sugars 5g	
Protein 29g	Fat 13g	
Carbohydrate 11g	Saturates 3g	

🍖 10 MINS   🕐 10 MINS

SERVES 4

I N G R E D I E N T S

4 boneless, skinless chicken breasts

1 egg white

2 tbsp sesame seeds

2 tbsp vegetable oil

1 onion, sliced

1 tbsp brown crystal
sugar

finely grated zest and juice of
1 lemon

3 tbsp lemon curd

7 oz can water chestnuts,
drained

lemon zest, to garnish

COOK'S TIP

Water chestnuts are commonly added to Chinese recipes for their crunchy texture as they do not have a great deal of flavor.

1 Place the chicken breasts between 2 sheets of plastic wrap and pound with a rolling pin to flatten. Slice the chicken into thin strips.

2 Whisk the egg white until light and foamy. Dip the chicken strips into the egg white, then coat in the sesame seeds.

3 Heat the oil in a wok and stir-fry the onion for 2 minutes until softened.

4 Add the chicken to the wok and stir-fry for 5 minutes, or until the chicken turns golden.

5 Mix the sugar, lemon zest, lemon juice and lemon curd and add to the wok. Allow it to bubble slightly.

6 Slice the water chestnuts thinly, add to the wok and cook for 2 minutes. Garnish with lemon zest and serve hot.

Cashew Chicken

Yellow bean sauce is available from large supermarkets. Try to buy a chunky sauce rather than a smooth sauce for texture.

NUTRITIONAL INFORMATION

Calories . . . . . . .398 Sugars 2g
Protein . . . . .31g Fat 27g
Carbohydrate . . . .8g Saturates 4g

 10 MINS   15 MINS

SERVES 4

INGREDIENTS

1 lb boneless chicken breasts

2 tbsp vegetable oil

1 red onion, sliced

1½ cups flat mushrooms, sliced

⅓ cup cashew nuts

2¾ oz jar yellow bean sauce

fresh cilantro, to garnish

egg fried rice or plain boiled rice, to serve

1 Using a sharp knife, remove the excess skin from the chicken breasts, if desired. Cut the chicken into small, bite-sized chunks.

2 Heat the vegetable oil in a preheated wok or skillet.

3 Add the chicken to the wok and stir-fry for 5 minutes.

4 Add the red onion and mushrooms to the wok and continue to stir-fry for a further 5 minutes.

5 Place the cashew nuts on a cookie sheet and toast under a preheated medium broiler until just browning – toasting nuts brings out their flavor.

6 Toss the toasted cashew nuts into the wok together with the yellow bean sauce and heat through.

7 Allow the sauce to bubble for 2–3 minutes.

8 Transfer the chop suey to warm serving bowls and garnish with fresh cilantro. Serve hot with egg fried rice or plain boiled rice.

VARIATION

Chicken thighs could be used instead of the chicken breasts for a more economical dish.

Chicken Foo-Yong

Although commonly described as an omelet, a foo-yong ('white lotus petals') should use egg whites only to create a very delicate texture.

NUTRITIONAL INFORMATION

Calories ....220 Sugars 1g
Protein ....16g Fat 14g
Carbohydrate ....7g Saturates 3g

  5 MINS   🕐 5 MINS

SERVES 4

I N G R E D I E N T S

6 oz chicken breast fillet, skinned

½ tsp salt

pepper

1 tsp rice wine or dry sherry

1 tbsp cornstarch

3 eggs

½ tsp finely chopped scallions

3 tbsp vegetable oil

4½ oz green peas

1 tsp light soy sauce

salt

few drops of sesame oil

1 Cut the chicken across the grain into very small, paper-thin slices, using a cleaver. Place the chicken slices in a shallow dish.

2 In a small bowl, mix together ½ teaspoon salt, pepper, rice wine or dry sherry and cornstarch.

3 Pour the mixture over the chicken slices in the dish, turning the chicken until well coated.

4 Beat the eggs in a small bowl with a pinch of salt and the scallions.

5 Heat the vegetable oil in a preheated wok, add the chicken slices and stir-fry for about 1 minute, making sure that the slices are kept separated.

6 Pour the beaten eggs over the chicken, and lightly scramble until set. Do not stir too vigorously, or the mixture will break up in the oil. Stir the oil from the bottom of the wok so that the foo-yong rises to the surface.

7 Add the peas, light soy sauce and salt to taste and blend well. Transfer to warm serving dishes, sprinkle with sesame oil and serve.

COOK'S TIP

If available, chicken *goujons* can be used for this dish: these are small, delicate strips of chicken which require no further cutting and are very tender.

Sweet & Sour Pork

This dish is a popular choice in Western diets, and must be one of the best known of Chinese recipes.

NUTRITIONAL INFORMATION

Calories 471	Sugars 47g
Protein 16g	Fat 13g
Carbohydrate . . .77g	Saturates 2g

 10 MINS   🕐 20 MINS

SERVES 4

I N G R E D I E N T S

⅔ cup vegetable oil, for deep-frying

8 oz pork tenderloin, cut into ½-inch cubes

1 onion, sliced

1 green bell pepper, seeded and sliced

8 oz pineapple pieces

1 small carrot, cut into thin strips

1 oz canned bamboo shoots,
   drained, rinsed and halved

rice or noodles, to serve

B A T T E R

1 cup all-purpose flour

1 tbsp cornstarch

1½ tsp baking powder

1 tbsp vegetable oil

S A U C E

⅔ cup light brown sugar

2 tbsp cornstarch

½ cup white wine vinegar

2 garlic cloves, crushed

4 tbsp tomato paste

6 tbsp pineapple juice

1 To make the batter, sift the all-purpose flour into a mixing bowl, together with the cornstarch and baking powder. Add the vegetable oil and stir in enough water to make a thick, smooth batter (about ¾ cup).

2 Pour the vegetable oil into a preheated wok and heat until almost smoking.

3 Dip the cubes of pork into the batter, and cook in the hot oil, in batches, until the pork is cooked through. Remove the pork from the wok with a slotted spoon and drain on absorbent paper towels. Set aside and keep warm until required.

4 Drain all but 1 tablespoon of oil from the wok and return it to the heat. Add the onion, bell pepper, pineapple pieces, carrot and bamboo shoots and stir-fry for 1–2 minutes. Remove from the wok with a slotted spoon and set aside.

5 Mix all of the sauce ingredients together and pour into the wok. Bring to the boil, stirring until thickened and clear. Cook for 1 minute, then return the pork and vegetables to the wok. Cook for a further 1–2 minutes, then transfer to a serving plate and serve with rice or noodles.

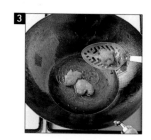

Meatballs in Peanut Sauce

Choose very lean ground beef to make these meatballs – or better still, buy some lean beef and grind it yourself.

NUTRITIONAL INFORMATION

Calories 553	Sugars 10g	
Protein 32g	Fat 43g	
Carbohydrate ...21g	Saturates 12g	

5 MINS   30 MINS

SERVES 4

INGREDIENTS

2 cups lean ground beef

2 tsp finely grated fresh ginger

1 small red chili, deseeded and chopped finely

1 tbsp chopped fresh basil or cilantro

1 tbsp sesame oil

1 tbsp vegetable oil

salt and pepper

SAUCE

2 tbsp red curry paste

1¼ cups coconut milk

1 cup ground peanuts

1 tbsp fish sauce

TO GARNISH

chopped fresh basil

sprigs of fresh basil or cilantro

1 Put the beef, ginger, chili and basil or cilantro into a food processor or blender. Add $^1/_2$ teaspoon of salt and plenty of pepper. Process for about 10–15 seconds until finely chopped. Alternatively, chop the ingredients finely and mix together.

2 Form the beef mixture into about 12 balls. Heat the sesame oil and vegetable oil in a wok or skillet and fry the meatballs over a medium-high heat until well browned on all sides, about 10 minutes. Lift them out and drain on paper towels.

3 To make the sauce, stir-fry the red curry paste in the wok or skillet for 1 minute. Add the coconut milk, peanuts and fish sauce. Heat, stirring, until just simmering.

4 Return the meatballs to the wok or skillet and cook gently in the sauce for 10–15 minutes. If the sauce begins to get too thick, add a little extra coconut milk or water. Season with a little salt and pepper, according to taste.

5 Serve garnished with chopped fresh basil and sprigs of fresh basil or cilantro.

VARIATION

Ground lamb makes a delicious alternative to beef. If you do use lamb, try substituting ground almonds for the peanuts and fresh mint for the basil.

Beef & Beans

The green of the beans complements the dark color of the beef, served in a rich sauce.

NUTRITIONAL INFORMATION

Calories 381	Sugars 3g	
Protein 25g	Fat 27g	
Carbohydrate . . .10g	Saturates 8g	

 35 MINS   15 MINS

SERVES 4

I N G R E D I E N T S

1 lb rump or fillet steak, cut into 1-inch pieces

M A R I N A D E

2 tsp cornstarch

2 tbsp dark soy sauce

2 tsp peanut oil

S A U C E

2 tbsp vegetable oil

3 garlic cloves, crushed

1 small onion, cut into 8

8 oz thin green beans, halved

¼ cup unsalted cashews

1 oz canned bamboo shoots, drained and rinsed

2 tsp dark soy sauce

2 tsp Chinese rice wine or dry sherry

½ cup beef stock

2 tsp cornstarch

4 tsp water

salt and pepper

1 To make the marinade, mix together the cornstarch, soy sauce and peanut oil.

2 Place the steak in a shallow glass bowl. Pour the marinade over the steak, turn to coat thoroughly, cover and leave to marinate in the refrigerator for at least 30 minutes.

3 To make the sauce, heat the oil in a preheated wok. Add the garlic, onion, beans, cashews and bamboo shoots and stir-fry for 2–3 minutes.

4 Remove the steak from the marinade, drain, add to the wok and stir-fry for 3–4 minutes.

5 Mix the soy sauce, Chinese rice wine or sherry and beef stock together. Blend the cornstarch with the water and add to the soy sauce mixture, mixing to combine.

6 Stir the mixture into the wok and bring the sauce to the boil, stirring until thickened and clear. Reduce the heat and leave to simmer for 2–3 minutes. Season to taste and serve immediately.

Soy & Sesame Beef

Soy sauce and sesame seeds are classic ingredients in Chinese cookery.
Use a dark soy sauce for fuller flavor and richness.

NUTRITIONAL INFORMATION

Calories	...... .324	Sugars	..........2g
Protein	........25g	Fat	..........22g
Carbohydrate	....3g	Saturates	........6g

 5 MINS   10 MINS

SERVES 4

I N G R E D I E N T S

2 tbsp sesame seeds

1 lb beef fillet

2 tbsp vegetable oil

1 green bell pepper, deseeded and thinly
   sliced

4 cloves garlic, crushed

2 tbsp dry sherry

4 tbsp soy sauce

6 scallions, sliced

noodles, to serve

1 Heat a large wok or heavy-based
skillet until it is very hot.

2 Add the sesame seeds to the wok or
skillet and dry fry, stirring, for 1–2
minutes or until they just begin to brown.
Remove the sesame seeds from the wok
and set aside until required.

3 Using a sharp knife or meat cleaver,
thinly slice the beef.

4 Heat the vegetable oil in the wok or
skillet. Add the beef and stir-fry for
2–3 minutes or until sealed on all sides.

5 Add the sliced bell pepper and
crushed garlic to the wok and
continue stir-frying for 2 minutes.

6 Add the dry sherry and soy sauce to
the wok together with the scallions.
Allow the mixture in the wok to bubble,
stirring occasionally, for about 1 minute,
but do not let the mixture burn.

7 Transfer the garlic beef stir-fry to
warm serving bowls and scatter with
the dry-fried sesame seeds. Serve hot with
boiled noodles.

COOK'S TIP

You can spread the
sesame seeds out on a cookie
sheet and toast them under a
preheated broiler until browned
all over, if you prefer.

Seafood Omelet

This delicious omelet is filled with a mixture of fresh vegetables, sliced squid and shrimp.

NUTRITIONAL INFORMATION

Calories 216	Sugars 2g	
Protein 20g	Fat 13g	
Carbohydrate 4g	Saturates 4g	

5 MINS   10 MINS

SERVES 4

I N G R E D I E N T S

4 eggs

3 tbsp milk

1 tbsp fish sauce or light soy sauce

1 tbsp sesame oil

3 shallots, sliced finely

1 small red bell pepper, cored, deseeded and sliced very finely

1 small leek, trimmed and cut into matchstick pieces

125 g/4½ oz squid rings

⅔ cup cooked peeled shrimp

1 tbsp chopped fresh basil

1 tbsp butter

salt and pepper

sprigs of fresh basil, to garnish

1 Beat the eggs, milk and fish sauce or soy sauce together.

2 Heat the sesame oil in a wok or large skillet and add the shallots, bell pepper and leek. Stir-fry briskly for 2–3 minutes.

3 Add the squid rings, shrimp and chopped basil to the wok or skillet. Stir-fry for a further 2–3 minutes, until the squid looks opaque.

4 Season the mixture in the wok with salt and pepper to taste. Transfer to a warmed plate and keep warm until required.

5 Melt the butter in a large omelet pan or skillet and add the beaten egg mixture. Cook over a medium-high heat until just set.

6 Spoon the vegetable and seafood mixture in a line down the middle of the omelet, then fold each side of the omelet over.

7 Transfer the omelet to a warmed serving dish and cut into 4 portions. Garnish with sprigs of fresh basil and serve at once.

VARIATION

Chopped, cooked chicken makes a delicious alternative to the squid.

Use fresh cilantro instead of the basil, if desired.

Trout with Pineapple

Pineapple is widely used in Chinese cooking. The tartness of fresh pineapple complements fish particularly well.

NUTRITIONAL INFORMATION

Calories 243	Sugars 4g
Protein 30g	Fat 11g
Carbohydrate 6g	Saturates 2g

5 MINS   15 MINS

SERVES 4

I N G R E D I E N T S

4 trout fillets, skinned

2 tbsp vegetable oil

2 garlic cloves, cut into slivers

4 slices fresh pineapple, peeled and diced

1 celery stalk, sliced

1 tbsp light soy sauce

¼ cup fresh or unsweetened pineapple juice

⅔ cup fish stock

1 tsp cornstarch

2 tsp water

shredded celery leaves and fresh red chili slices, to garnish

1 Cut the trout fillets into strips. Heat 1 tablespoon of the vegetable oil in a preheated wok until almost smoking. Reduce the heat slightly, add the fish and sauté for 2 minutes. Remove from the wok and set aside.

2 Add the remaining oil to the wok, reduce the heat and add the garlic, diced pineapple and celery. Stir-fry for 1–2 minutes.

3 Add the soy sauce, pineapple juice and fish stock to the wok. Bring to the boil and cook, stirring, for 2–3 minutes, or until the sauce has reduced.

4 Blend the cornstarch with the water to form a paste and stir it into the wok. Bring the sauce to the boil and cook, stirring constantly, until the sauce thickens and clears.

5 Return the fish to the wok, and cook, stirring gently, until heated through. Transfer to a warmed serving dish and serve, garnished with shredded celery leaves and red chili slices.

VARIATION

Use canned pineapple instead of fresh pineapple if you wish, choosing slices in unsweetened, natural juice in preference to a syrup.

Fish with Ginger Butter

Whole mackerel or trout are stuffed with herbs, wrapped in foil, baked and then drizzled with a fresh ginger butter.

NUTRITIONAL INFORMATION

Calories 328	Sugar 0g	
Protein 24g	Fat 25g	
Carbohydrate 1g	Saturates 13g	

 10 MINS   🕐 30 MINS

SERVES 4

INGREDIENTS

4 x 9 oz whole trout or mackerel, gutted

4 tbsp chopped fresh cilantro

5 garlic cloves, crushed

2 tsp grated lemon or lime zest

2 tsp vegetable oil

banana leaves, for wrapping (optional)

6 tbsp butter

1 tbsp grated fresh ginger

1 tbsp light soy sauce

salt and pepper

cilantro sprigs and lemon or lime wedges, to garnish

1 Wash and dry the fish. Mix the cilantro with the garlic, lemon or lime zest and salt and pepper to taste. Spoon into the fish cavities.

2 Brush the fish with a little oil, season well and place each fish on a double thickness sheet of baking parchment or foil and wrap up well to enclose. Alternatively, wrap in banana leaves.

3 Place on a cookie sheet and bake in a preheated oven for about 25 minutes or until the flesh will flake easily.

4 Meanwhile, melt the butter in a small pan. Add the ginger and mix well.

5 Stir the light soy sauce into the saucepan.

6 To serve, unwrap the fish parcels, drizzle over the ginger butter and garnish with cilantro and lemon or lime wedges.

COOK'S TIP

For a really authentic touch, wrap the fish in banana leaves, which can be ordered from specialist oriental stores. They are not edible, but impart a delicate flavor to the fish.

Seafood Medley

Use any combination of fish and seafood in this delicious dish of coated fish served in a wine sauce.

NUTRITIONAL INFORMATION

Calories 168   Sugars 2g

Protein . . . . .29g   Fat 3g

Carbohydrate . . . .4g   Saturates 1g

5 MINS   15 MINS

SERVES 4

INGREDIENTS

2 tbsp dry white wine

1 egg white, lightly beaten

½ tsp Chinese five-spice powder

1 tsp cornstarch

10½ oz raw shrimp,
    peeled and deveined

4½ oz prepared squid,
    cut into rings

4½ oz white fish fillets,
    cut into strips

vegetable oil, for deep-frying

1 green bell pepper, seeded and
    cut into thin strips

1 carrot, cut into thin strips

4 baby corn cobs, halved lengthways

1 Mix the wine, egg white, five-spice powder and cornstarch in a large bowl. Add the shrimp, squid rings and fish fillets and stir to coat evenly. Remove the fish and seafood with a slotted spoon, reserving any leftover cornstarch mixture.

2 Heat the oil in a preheated wok and deep-fry the shrimp, squid and fish for 2–3 minutes. Remove the seafood mixture from the wok with a slotted spoon and set aside.

3 Pour off all but 1 tablespoon of oil from the wok and return to the heat. Add the bell pepper, carrot and corn cobs and stir-fry for 4–5 minutes.

4 Return the seafood to the wok with any remaining cornstarch mixture. Heat through, stirring, and serve.

COOK'S TIP

Open up the squid rings and using a sharp knife, score a lattice pattern on the flesh to make them look attractive.

Prawns with Vegetables

This colorful and delicious dish is cooked with vegetables: vary them according to seasonal availability.

NUTRITIONAL INFORMATION

Calories . . . . . . .298 Sugars 1g
Protein . . . . .13g Fat 26g
Carbohydrate . . . .3g Saturates 3g

5 MINS   10 MINS

SERVES 4

INGREDIENTS

2 oz snow peas

½ small carrot

2 oz baby corn cobs

2 oz straw mushrooms

6-9 oz raw jumbo shrimp, peeled

1 tsp salt

½ egg white, lightly beaten

1 tsp cornstarch paste

about 1¼ cups
     vegetable oil

1 scallion, cut into
     short sections

4 slices fresh ginger, peeled and finely
     chopped

½ tsp sugar

1 tbsp light soy sauce

1 tsp Chinese rice wine or dry sherry

a few drops sesame oil

lemon slices and chopped fresh chives,
     to garnish

1 Using a sharp knife, top and tail the snow peas; cut the carrot into the same size as the snow peas; halve the baby corncobs and straw mushrooms.

2 Mix the shrimp with a pinch of the salt, the egg white and cornstarch paste until the shrimp are evenly coated.

3 Preheat a wok over a high heat for 2-3 minutes, then add the vegetable oil and heat to medium-hot.

4 Add the shrimp to the wok, stirring to separate them. Remove the shrimp with a slotted spoon as soon as the color changes.

5 Pour off the oil, leaving about 1 tablespoon in the wok. Add the snow peas, carrot, corncobs, mushrooms and scallions.

6 Add the shrimp together with the ginger, sugar, soy sauce and wine or sherry, blending well.

7 Sprinkle with the sesame oil and serve hot, garnished with lemon slices and chopped fresh chives.

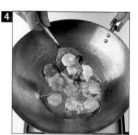

Fish with Black Bean Sauce

Steaming is one of the preferred methods of cooking whole fish in China as it maintains both the flavor and the texture.

NUTRITIONAL INFORMATION

Calories 292   Sugars 3g
Protein . . . . .44g   Fat 7g
Carbohydrate . . . .6g   Saturates 0.4g

🕐 10 MINS   🕐 10 MINS

SERVES 4

I N G R E D I E N T S

2 lb whole snapper, cleaned and scaled

3 garlic cloves, crushed

2 tbsp black bean sauce

1 tsp cornstarch

2 tsp sesame oil

2 tbsp light soy sauce

2 tsp superfine sugar

2 tbsp dry sherry

1 small leek, shredded

1 small red bell pepper, seeded and cut into thin strips

shredded leek and lemon wedges, to garnish

boiled rice or noodles, to serve

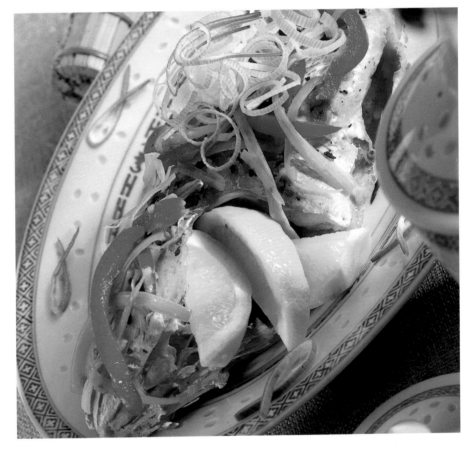

1 Rinse the fish inside and out with cold running water and pat dry with paper towels.

2 Make 2-3 diagonal slashes in the flesh on each side of the fish, using a sharp knife. Rub the garlic into the fish.

3 Mix together the black bean sauce, cornstarch, sesame oil, light soy sauce, sugar and dry sherry.

4 Place the fish in a shallow heatproof dish and pour the sauce mixture over the top. Sprinkle the shredded leek and bell pepper strips on top of the sauce.

5 Place the dish in the top of a steamer, cover and steam for 10 minutes, or until the fish is cooked through.

6 Transfer the fish to a serving dish, garnish with shredded leek and lemon wedges and serve with boiled rice or noodles.

COOK'S TIP

Insert the point of a sharp knife into the fish to test if it is cooked. The fish is cooked through if the knife goes into the flesh easily.

Mussels with Lemon Grass

Give fresh mussels a Far Eastern flavor by using some Kaffir lime leaves, garlic and lemon grass in the stock used for steaming them.

NUTRITIONAL INFORMATION

Calories 194   Sugar 0g
Protein ....33g   Fat 7g
Carbohydrate ....1g   Saturates 1g

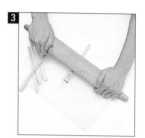

10 MINS   10 MINS

SERVES 4

INGREDIENTS

1 lb 10 oz live mussels

1 tbsp sesame oil

3 shallots, chopped finely

2 garlic cloves, chopped finely

1 stalk lemon grass

2 Kaffir lime leaves

2 tbsp chopped fresh cilantro

finely grated rind of 1 lime

2 tbsp lime juice

1¼ cups hot vegetable stock

crusty bread, to serve

fresh cilantro, to garnish

1 Using a small sharp knife, scrape the beards off the mussels under cold running water. Scrub them well, discarding any that are damaged or remain open when tapped. Keep rinsing until there is no trace of sand.

2 Heat the sesame oil in a large saucepan and fry the shallots and garlic gently until softened, about 2 minutes.

3 Bruise the lemon grass, using a meat mallet or rolling pin, and add to the pan with the Kaffir lime leaves, cilantro, lime rind and juice, mussels and stock. Put the lid on the saucepan and cook over a moderate heat for 3–5 minutes. Shake the pan from time to time.

4 Lift the mussels out into 4 warmed soup plates, discarding any that remain shut. Boil the remaining liquid rapidly to reduce slightly. Remove the lemon grass and lime leaves, then pour the liquid over the mussels.

5 Garnish with cilantro and lime wedges, and serve at once.

COOK'S TIP

Mussels are now farmed, so they should be available throughout the year.

Shrimp Stir-Fry

A very quick and tasty stir-fry using shrimp and cucumber, cooked with lemon grass, chili and ginger.

NUTRITIONAL INFORMATION

Calories	178	Sugars	.........1g
Protein	........22g	Fat	...........7g
Carbohydrate	....3g	Saturates	.......1g

5 MINS   5 MINS

SERVES 4

I N G R E D I E N T S

½ cucumber

2 tbsp sunflower oil

6 scallions, halved lengthways and cut into
    1½ inch lengths

1 stalk lemon grass, sliced thinly

1 garlic clove, chopped

1 tsp chopped fresh red chili

4½ oz oyster mushrooms

1 tsp chopped fresh ginger

12 oz cooked peeled shrimp

2 tsp cornstarch

2 tbsp water

1 tbsp dark soy sauce

½ tsp fish sauce

2 tbsp dry sherry or rice wine

boiled rice, to serve

1 Cut the cucumber into strips about ¼ x 1¾ inches.

2 Heat the sunflower oil in a wok or large skillet.

3 Add the scallions, cucumber, lemon grass, garlic, chili, oyster mushrooms and ginger to the wok or skillet and stir-fry for 2 minutes.

4 Add the shrimp and stir-fry for a further minute.

5 Mix together the cornstarch, water, soy sauce and fish sauce until smooth.

6 Stir the cornstarch mixture and sherry or wine into the wok and heat through, stirring, until the sauce has thickened. Serve with rice.

COOK'S TIP

The white part of the lemon grass stem can be thinly sliced and left in the cooked dish. If using the whole stem, remove it before serving. You can buy lemon grass chopped and dried, or preserved in jars, but neither has the fragrance or delicacy of the fresh variety.

Mullet with Ginger

Ginger is used widely in Chinese cooking for its strong, pungent flavor. Although fresh ginger is best, ground ginger may be used instead.

NUTRITIONAL INFORMATION

Calories 195   Sugars 6g
Protein . . . . .31g   Fat 3g
Carbohydrate . . . .9g   Saturates 0g

   10 MINS   15 MINS

SERVES 4

I N G R E D I E N T S

1 whole mullet, cleaned and scaled

2 scallions, chopped

1 tsp grated fresh ginger

½ cup garlic wine vinegar

½ cup light soy sauce

3 tsp superfine sugar

dash of chili sauce

½ cup fish stock

1 green bell pepper, seeded and thinly sliced

1 large tomato, skinned, seeded and cut into thin strips

salt and pepper

sliced tomato, to garnish

1 Rinse the fish inside and out and pat dry with paper towels.

2 Make 3 diagonal slits in the flesh on each side of the fish. Season the fish with salt and pepper inside and out, according to taste.

3 Place the fish on a heatproof plate and scatter the chopped scallions and grated ginger over the top. Cover and steam for 10 minutes, or until the fish is cooked through.

4 Meanwhile, place the garlic wine vinegar, light soy sauce, superfine sugar, chili sauce, fish stock, bell pepper and tomato in a saucepan and bring to the boil, stirring occasionally.

5 Cook the sauce over a high heat until the sauce has slightly reduced and thickened.

6 Remove the fish from the steamer and transfer to a warm serving dish. Pour the sauce over the fish, garnish with tomato slices and serve immediately.

VARIATION

Use fillets of fish for this recipe if preferred, and reduce the cooking time to 5–7 minutes.

Shrimp & Corn Patties

Chopped small shrimps and corn are combined in a light batter, which is dropped into hot fat to make these tasty patties.

NUTRITIONAL INFORMATION

Calories 250	Sugars 1g
Protein 17g	Fat 9g
Carbohydrate ...26g	Saturates 2g

🍲 35 MINS   🕐 20 MINS

SERVES 4

INGREDIENTS

1 cup all-purpose flour

1½ tsp baking powder

2 eggs

about 1 cup cold water

1 garlic clove, very finely chopped

3 scallions, trimmed and very finely chopped

1 cup peeled small shrimp, chopped

½ cup canned corn, drained

vegetable oil for frying

salt and pepper

TO GARNISH

scallion brushes

lime slices

1 chili flower

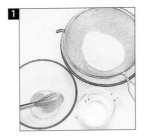  

1 Sift the flour, baking powder and ½ tsp salt into a bowl. Add the eggs and half the water and beat to make a smooth batter, adding extra water to give the consistency of heavy cream. Add the garlic and scallions. Cover and leave for 30 minutes.

2 Stir the small shrimp and corn into the batter. Season with pepper.

3 Heat 2–3 tablespoons of oil in a wok. Drop tablespoonfuls of the batter into the wok and cook over a medium heat until bubbles rise and the surface just sets. Flip the patties over and cook the other side until golden brown. Drain on paper towels.

4 Cook the remaining batter in the same way, adding more oil to the wok if required. Garnish and serve at once.

COOK'S TIP

To make chili flowers or scallion brushes hold the stem and cut down its length several times with a sharp knife. Place in a bowl of chilled water so that the 'petals' turn out. Remove the chili seeds when the 'petals' have opened.

Fried Squid Flowers

The addition of green bell pepper and black bean sauce to the squid makes a colorful and delicious dish from the Cantonese school.

NUTRITIONAL INFORMATION

Calories 172	Sugars 1g
Protein 13g	Fat 13g
Carbohydrate 2g	Saturates 1g

 10 MINS   5 MINS

SERVES 4

I N G R E D I E N T S

12-14 oz prepared and cleaned squid (see Cook's Tip, below)

1 medium green bell pepper, cored and seeded

3-4 tbsp vegetable oil

1 garlic clove, finely chopped

¼ tsp finely chopped ginger root

2 tsp finely chopped scallions

½ tsp salt

2 tbsp crushed black bean sauce

1 tsp Chinese rice wine or dry sherry

a few drops sesame oil

boiled rice, to serve

1 If ready-prepared squid is not available, prepare as instructed in the Cook's Tip, below.

2 Open up the squid and, using a meat cleaver or sharp knife, score the inside of the flesh in a criss-cross pattern.

3 Cut the squid into pieces about the size of an oblong postage stamp.

4 Blanch the squid pieces in a bowl of boiling water for a few seconds. Remove and drain; dry well on absorbent paper towels.

5 Cut the bell pepper into small triangular pieces. Heat the oil in a preheated wok or large skillet and stir-fry the bell pepper for about 1 minute.

6 Add the garlic, ginger, scallion, salt and squid. Continue stirring for another minute.

7 Finally add the black bean sauce and Chinese rice wine or dry sherry, and blend well.

8 Transfer the squid flowers to a serving dish, sprinkle with sesame oil and serve with boiled rice.

COOK'S TIP

Clean the squid by first cutting off the head. Cut off the tentacles and reserve. Remove the small soft bone at the base of the tentacles and the transparent backbone, as well as the ink bag. Peel off the thin skin, then wash and dry well.

Scallop Pancakes

Scallops, like most shellfish require very little cooking, and this original dish is a perfect example of how to use shellfish to its full potential.

NUTRITIONAL INFORMATION

Calories ....240 Sugars 1g
Protein ....29g Fat 9g
Carbohydrate ....11g Saturates 1g

5 MINS   30 MINS

SERVES 4

INGREDIENTS

3½ oz fine green beans

1 red chili

1 lb scallops, without roe

1 egg

3 scallions, sliced

½ cup rice flour

1 tbsp fish sauce

oil, for frying

salt

sweet chili dip, to serve

1 Using a sharp knife, trim the green beans and slice them very thinly.

2 Using a sharp knife, deseed and very finely chop the red chili.

3 Bring a small saucepan of lightly salted water to the boil. Add the green beans to the pan and cook for 3–4 minutes or until just softened.

4 Roughly chop the scallops and place them in a large bowl. Add the cooked beans to the scallops.

5 Mix the egg with the scallions, rice flour, fish sauce and chili until well combined. Add to the scallops and mix well.

6 Heat about 1 inch of oil in a large preheated wok. Add a ladleful of the mixture to the wok and cook for 5 minutes until golden and set.

7 Remove the pancake from the wok and leave to drain on absorbent paper towels. Keep warm while cooking the remaining pancake mixture. Serve the pancakes hot with a sweet chili dip.

VARIATION

You could use shrimp or shelled clams instead of the scallops, if you prefer.

Sweet & Sour Cauliflower

Although sweet and sour flavorings are mainly associated with pork, they are ideal for flavoring vegetables as in this tasty recipe.

NUTRITIONAL INFORMATION

Calories 154   Sugars 16g
Protein ....6g   Fat 7g
Carbohydrate ...17g   Saturates 1g

 5 MINS   20 MINS

SERVES 4

INGREDIENTS

1 lb cauliflower florets

2 tbsp sunflower oil

1 onion, sliced

8 oz carrots, sliced

3½ oz snow peas

1 ripe mango, sliced

1 cup bean sprouts

3 tbsp chopped fresh cilantro

3 tbsp fresh lime juice

1 tbsp clear honey

6 tbsp coconut milk

1 Bring a large saucepan of water to the boil. Add the cauliflower to the pan and cook for 2 minutes. Drain the cauliflower thoroughly.

2 Heat the sunflower oil in a large preheated wok.

3 Add the onion and carrots to the wok and stir-fry for about 5 minutes.

4 Add the drained cauliflower and snow peas to the wok and stir-fry for 2–3 minutes.

5 Add the mango and bean sprouts to the wok and stir-fry for about 2 minutes.

6 Mix together the cilantro, lime juice, honey and coconut milk in a bowl.

7 Add the cilantro and coconut mixture to the wok and stir-fry for about 2 minutes or until the juices are bubbling.

8 Transfer the sweet and sour cauliflower stir-fry to serving dishes and serve immediately.

VARIATION

Use broccoli instead of the cauliflower as an alternative, if you prefer.

Honey-Fried Chinese Cabbage

Chinese cabbage are rather similar to lettuce in that the leaves are delicate with a sweet flavor.

NUTRITIONAL INFORMATION

Calories 121	Sugars 6g	
Protein 5g	Fat 7g	
Carbohydrate . . .10g	Saturates 1g	

5 MINS | 10 MINS

SERVES 4

I N G R E D I E N T S

1 lb Chinese cabbage

1 tbsp peanut oil

½-inch piece fresh ginger, grated

2 garlic cloves, crushed

1 fresh red chili, sliced

1 tbsp Chinese rice wine or dry sherry

4½ tsp light soy sauce

1 tbsp clear honey

½ cup orange juice

1 tbsp sesame oil

2 tsp sesame seeds

orange zest, to garnish

COOK'S TIP

Single-flower honey has a better, more individual flavor than blended honey. Acacia honey is typically Chinese, but you could also try clover, lemon blossom, lime flower or orange blossom.

1 Separate the Chinese cabbage and shred finely, using a sharp knife.

2 Heat the peanut oil in a preheated wok. Add the ginger, garlic and chili to the wok and stir-fry the mixture for about 30 seconds.

3 Add the Chinese cabbage, Chinese rice wine or sherry, soy sauce, honey and orange juice to the wok. Reduce the heat and leave to simmer for 5 minutes.

4 Add the sesame oil to the wok, sprinkle the sesame seeds on top and mix to combine.

5 Transfer to a warm serving dish, garnish with the orange zest and serve immediately.

Spicy Eggplant

Try to obtain the smaller Chinese eggplants for this dish, as they have a slightly sweeter taste.

NUTRITIONAL INFORMATION

Calories 120   Sugars 7g
Protein ....2g   Fat 9g
Carbohydrate ....9g   Saturates 1g

 35 MINS   20 MINS

SERVES 4

INGREDIENTS

1 lb eggplant, rinsed

2 tsp salt

3 tbsp vegetable oil

2 garlic cloves, crushed

1-inch piece fresh ginger, chopped

1 onion, halved and sliced

1 fresh red chili, sliced

2 tbsp dark soy sauce

1 tbsp hoisin sauce

½ tsp chili sauce

1 tbsp dark brown sugar

1 tbsp wine vinegar

1 tsp ground Szechuan pepper

1¼ cups vegetable stock

1 Cut the eggplant into cubes if you are using the larger variety, or cut the smaller type in half. Place in a colander and sprinkle with the salt. Let stand for 30 minutes. Rinse under cold running water and pat dry with paper towels.

2 Heat the oil in a preheated wok and add the garlic, ginger, onion and fresh chili. Stir-fry for 30 seconds and add the eggplant. Continue to cook for 1–2 minutes.

3 Add the soy sauce, hoisin sauce, chili sauce, sugar, wine vinegar, Szechuan pepper and vegetable stock to the wok, reduce the heat and leave to simmer, uncovered, for 10 minutes, or until the eggplant are cooked.

4 Increase the heat and boil to reduce the sauce until thickened enough to coat the eggplant. Serve immediately.

COOK'S TIP

Sprinkling the eggplant with salt and letting them stand removes the bitter juices, which would otherwise taint the flavor of the dish.

Lemon Chinese Cabbage

This stir-fried Chinese cabbage is served with a tangy sauce made of grated lemon rind, lemon juice and ginger.

NUTRITIONAL INFORMATION

Calories 120	Sugars 0g
Protein 5g	Fat 8g
Carbohydrate 8g	Saturates 1g

5 MINS   10 MINS

SERVES 4

I N G R E D I E N T S

1 lb 2 oz Chinese cabbage

3 tbsp vegetable oil

½ inch piece fresh ginger, grated

1 tsp salt

1 tsp sugar

½ cup water or vegetable stock

1 tsp grated lemon rind

1 tbsp cornstarch

1 tbsp lemon juice

1 Separate the Chinese cabbage, wash and drain thoroughly. Pat dry with absorbent paper towels.

2 Cut the Chinese cabbage into 2 inch wide slices.

3 Heat the oil in a wok and add the grated fresh ginger followed by the Chinese cabbage, stir-fry for 2–3 minutes or until the leaves begin to wilt.

4 Add the salt and sugar, and mix well until the leaves soften. Remove the leaves with a slotted spoon and set aside.

5 Add the water or stock to the wok with the lemon rind. Bring to the boil.

6 Meanwhile, mix the cornstarch to a smooth paste with the lemon juice, then add to the wok. Simmer, stirring constantly, for about 1 minute to make a smooth sauce.

7 Return the cooked Chinese cabbage to the pan and mix thoroughly to coat the leaves in the sauce. Arrange on a serving plate and serve immediately.

COOK'S TIP

If Chinese cabbage is unavailable, substitute slices of savoy cabbage. Cook for 1 extra minute to soften the leaves.

Broccoli & Black Bean Sauce

Broccoli works well with the black bean sauce in this recipe, while the almonds add extra crunch and flavor.

NUTRITIONAL INFORMATION

Calories 139	Sugars 3g	
Protein 7g	Fat 10g	
Carbohydrate 5g	Saturates 1g	

 5 MINS   15 MINS

SERVES 4

INGREDIENTS

1 lb broccoli florets

2 tbsp sunflower oil

1 onion, sliced

2 cloves garlic, thinly sliced

¼ cup slivered almonds

1 head Chinese cabbage, shredded

4 tbsp black bean sauce

1 Bring a large saucepan of water to the boil.

2 Add the broccoli florets to the pan and cook for 1 minute. Drain the broccoli thoroughly.

3 Meanwhile, heat the sunflower oil in a large preheated wok.

4 Add the onion and garlic slices to the wok and stir-fry until just beginning to brown.

5 Add the drained broccoli florets and the slivered almonds to the mixture in the wok and stir-fry for a further 2–3 minutes.

6 Add the shredded Chinese cabbage to the wok and stir-fry for a further 2 minutes, stirring the leaves briskly around the wok.

7 Stir the black bean sauce into the vegetables in the wok, tossing to coat the vegetables thoroughly in the sauce and cook until the juices are just beginning to bubble.

8 Transfer the vegetables to warm serving bowls and serve immediately.

VARIATION

Use unsalted cashew nuts instead of the almonds, if preferred.

Caraway Cabbage

This makes a delicious vegetable accompaniment to all types of food: it can also be served as a vegetarian main dish.

NUTRITIONAL INFORMATION

Calories ....223 Sugars 17g
Protein ....6g Fat 14g
Carbohydrate ...18g Saturates 1g

5 MINS   10 MINS

SERVES 4

I N G R E D I E N T S

1 lb 2 oz white cabbage

1 tbsp sunflower oil

4 scallions, thinly sliced diagonally

6 tbsp raisins

½ cup walnut pieces or pecan nuts, roughly chopped

5 tbsp milk or vegetable stock

1 tbsp caraway seeds

1-2 tbsp freshly chopped mint

salt and pepper

mint sprigs, to garnish

1 Remove any outer leaves from the cabbage and cut out the stem, then shred the leaves very finely, either by hand or using the fine slicing blade on a food processor.

2 Heat the sunflower oil in a wok, swirling it around until it is really hot.

3 Add the scallions to the wok and stir-fry for a minute or so.

4 Add the shredded cabbage and stir-fry for 3–4 minutes, keeping the cabbage moving all the time and stirring from the outside to the centre of the wok. Make sure the cabbage does not stick to the wok or go brown.

5 Add the raisins, walnuts or pecans and milk or vegetable stock and continue to stir-fry for 3–4 minutes until the cabbage begins to soften slightly but is still crisp.

6 Season well with salt and pepper, add the caraway seeds and 1 tablespoon of the chopped mint and continue to stir-fry for a minute or so.

7 Serve sprinkled with the remaining chopped mint and garnish with sprigs of fresh mint.

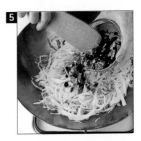

VARIATION

Red cabbage may be cooked in the same way in the wok, but substitute 2 tablespoons red or white wine vinegar and 3 tablespoons water for the milk and add 1 tablespoon brown sugar. Add a finely chopped dessert apple if liked.

Deep-Fried Zucchini

These zucchini fritters are irresistible and could be served as a starter or snack with a chili dip.

NUTRITIONAL INFORMATION

Calories 117   Sugars 2g
Protein . . . . .3g   Fat 6g
Carbohydrate . . .14g   Saturates 1g

 5 MINS   20 MINS

SERVES 4

INGREDIENTS

1 lb zucchini

1 egg white

⅓ cup cornstarch

1 tsp salt

1 tsp Chinese five-spice powder

oil, for deep-frying

chili dip, to serve

1 Using a sharp knife, slice the zucchini into rings or chunky sticks.

2 Place the egg white in a small mixing bowl. Lightly whip the egg white until foamy, using a fork.

3 Mix the cornstarch, salt and Chinese five-spice powder together and sprinkle on to a large plate.

4 Heat the oil for deep-frying in a large preheated wok or heavy-based skillet.

5 Dip each piece of zucchini into the beaten egg white then coat in the cornstarch and five-spice mixture.

6 Deep-fry the zucchini, in batches, for about 5 minutes or until pale golden and crispy. Repeat with the remaining zucchini.

7 Remove the zucchini with a slotted spoon and leave to drain on absorbent paper towels while deep-frying the remainder.

8 Transfer the zucchini to serving plates and serve immediately with a chili dip.

VARIATION

Alter the seasoning by using chili powder or curry powder instead of the Chinese five-spice powder, if you prefer.

Green & Black Bean Stir-Fry

A terrific side dish, the variety of greens in this recipe make it as attractive as it is tasty.

NUTRITIONAL INFORMATION

Calories 88   Sugars 2g
Protein . . . . .2g   Fat 7g
Carbohydrate . . . .4g   Saturates 4g

 5 MINS   10 MINS

SERVES 4

INGREDIENTS

8 oz fine green beans, sliced

4 shallots, sliced

3½ oz shiitake mushrooms, thinly sliced

1 clove garlic, crushed

1 Iceberg lettuce, shredded

1 tsp chili oil

2 tbsp butter

4 tbsp black bean sauce

1 Using a sharp knife, slice the fine green beans, shallots and shiitake mushrooms. Crush the garlic in a pestle and mortar and shred the Iceberg lettuce.

2 Heat the chili oil and butter in a large preheated wok or skillet.

3 Add the green beans, shallots, garlic and mushrooms to the wok and stir-fry for 2–3 minutes.

4 Add the shredded lettuce to the wok or skillet and stir-fry until the leaves have wilted.

5 Stir the black bean sauce into the mixture in the wok and heat through, tossing gently to mix, until the sauce is bubbling.

6 Transfer the green and black bean stir-fry to a warm serving dish and serve immediately.

COOK'S TIP

If possible, use Chinese green beans which are tender and can be eaten whole. They are available from specialist Chinese stores.

Bamboo with Spinach

In this recipe, spinach is fried with spices and then braised in a soy-flavored sauce with bamboo shoots for a rich, delicious dish.

NUTRITIONAL INFORMATION

Calories 105   Sugars 1g
Protein . . . . .3g   Fat 9g
Carbohydrate . . . .3g   Saturates 2g

 5 MINS   10 MINS

SERVES 4

I N G R E D I E N T S

3 tbsp peanut oil

8 oz spinach, chopped

6 oz canned bamboo shoots, drained and rinsed

1 garlic clove, crushed

2 fresh red chilies, sliced

pinch of ground cinnamon

1¼ cups vegetable stock

pinch of sugar

pinch of salt

1 tbsp light soy sauce

COOK'S TIP

Fresh bamboo shoots are rarely available in the West and, in any case, are extremely time-consuming to prepare. Canned bamboo shoots are quite satisfactory, as they are used to provide a crunchy texture, rather than for their flavor, which is fairly insipid.

1 Heat the peanut oil in a preheated wok or large skillet, swirling the oil around the base of the wok until it is really hot.

2 Add the spinach and bamboo shoots to the wok and stir-fry for 1 minute.

3 Add the garlic, chilies and cinnamon to the mixture in the wok and stir-fry for a further 30 seconds.

4 Stir in the stock, sugar, salt and light soy sauce, cover and cook over a medium heat for 5 minutes, or until the vegetables are cooked through and the sauce has reduced. If there is too much cooking liquid, blend a little cornstarch with double the quantity of cold water and stir into the sauce.

5 Transfer the bamboo shoots and spinach to a serving dish and serve.

Vegetable Chop Suey

Make sure that the vegetables are all cut into pieces of a similar size in this recipe, so that they cook within the same amount of time.

NUTRITIONAL INFORMATION

Calories 155   Sugars 6g
Protein . . . . .4g   Fat 12g
Carbohydrate . . . .9g   Saturates 2g

5 MINS   5 MINS

SERVES 4

I N G R E D I E N T S

1 yellow bell pepper, seeded

1 red bell pepper, seeded

1 carrot

1 zucchini

1 fennel bulb

1 onion

2 oz snow peas

2 tbsp peanut oil

3 garlic cloves, crushed

1 tsp grated fresh ginger

4½ oz bean sprouts

2 tsp light brown sugar

2 tbsp light soy sauce

½ cup vegetable stock

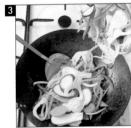

1 Cut the bell peppers, carrot, zucchini and fennel into thin slices. Cut the onion into quarters and then cut each quarter in half. Slice the snow peas diagonally to create the maximum surface area.

2 Heat the oil in a preheated wok, add the garlic and ginger and stir-fry for 30 seconds. Add the onion and stir-fry for a further 30 seconds.

3 Add the bell peppers, carrot, zucchini, fennel and snow peas to the wok and stir-fry for 2 minutes.

4 Add the bean sprouts to the wok and stir in the sugar, soy sauce and stock. Reduce the heat to low and simmer for 1–2 minutes, until the vegetables are tender and coated in the sauce.

5 Transfer the vegetables and sauce to a serving dish and serve immediately.

VARIATION

Use any combination of colorful vegetables that you have to hand to make this versatile dish.

Bean Curd with Mushrooms

Chunks of cucumber and smoked bean curd stir-fried with straw mushrooms, snow peas and corn in a yellow bean sauce.

NUTRITIONAL INFORMATION

Calories 130	Sugars 2g	
Protein 9g	Fat 9g	
Carbohydrate 3g	Saturates 1g	

 15 MINS   10 MINS

SERVES 4

INGREDIENTS

1 large cucumber

1 tsp salt

8 oz smoked bean curd

2 tbsp vegetable oil

60 g/2 oz snow peas

8 baby corn

1 celery stalk, sliced diagonally

15 oz can straw mushrooms, drained

2 scallions, cut into strips

½ inch piece ginger root, chopped

1 tbsp yellow bean sauce

1 tbsp light soy sauce

1 tbsp dry sherry

1 Halve the cucumber lengthways and remove the seeds, using a teaspoon or melon baller.

2 Cut the cucumber into cubes, place in a colander and sprinkle over the salt. Leave to drain for 10 minutes. Rinse thoroughly in cold water to remove the salt and drain thoroughly on absorbent paper towels.

3 Cut the bean curd into cubes.

4 Heat the vegetable oil in a wok or large skillet until smoking.

5 Add the bean curd, snow peas, baby corn and celery to the wok. Stir until the bean curd is lightly browned.

6 Add the straw mushrooms, scallions and ginger, and stir-fry for a further minute.

7 Stir in the cucumber, yellow bean sauce, light soy sauce, dry sherry and 2 tablespoons of water. Stir-fry for 1 minute and ensure that all the vegetables are coated in the sauces before serving.

COOK'S TIP

Straw mushrooms are available in cans from oriental suppliers and some supermarkets. If unavailable, substitute 9 oz baby button mushrooms.

Bean Curd with Hot & Sweet Sauce

Golden pieces of bean curd are served in a hot and creamy peanut and chili sauce for a classic vegetarian starter.

NUTRITIONAL INFORMATION

Calories 367	Sugars 5g
Protein 18g	Fat 30g
Carbohydrate 8g	Saturates 5g

5 MINS   15 MINS

SERVES 4

I N G R E D I E N T S

1 lb tofu bean curd, cubed

oil, for frying

S A U C E

6 tbsp crunchy peanut butter

1 tbsp sweet chili sauce

⅔ cup coconut milk

1 tbsp tomato paste

¼ cup chopped salted peanuts

1 Pat away any moisture from the bean curd, using absorbent paper towels.

2 Heat the oil in a large wok or skillet until very hot.

3 Add the bean curd to the wok and cook, in batches, for about 5 minutes, or until golden and crispy.

4 Remove the bean curd with a slotted spoon, transfer to absorbent paper towels and leave to drain.

5 To make the peanut and chili sauce, mix together the crunchy peanut butter, sweet chili sauce, coconut milk, tomato paste and chopped salted peanuts in a bowl. Add a little boiling water if necessary to achieve a smooth consistency. Stir well until the ingredients are thoroughly blended.

6 Transfer the bean curd to serving plates and pour the sauce over the top. Alternatively, pour the sauce into a serving dish and serve separately.

COOK'S TIP

Make sure that all of the moisture has been absorbed from the bean curd before frying, otherwise it will not crispen.

Cook the peanut and chili sauce in a saucepan over a gentle heat before serving, if you prefer.

Bean Curd Casserole

Bean curd is ideal for absorbing all the other flavors in this dish. If marinated bean curd is used, it will add a flavor of its own.

NUTRITIONAL INFORMATION

Calories ....228 Sugars 3g
Protein ....16g Fat 15g
Carbohydrate ....7g Saturates 2g

5 MINS   15 MINS

SERVES 4

I N G R E D I E N T S

1 lb bean curd

2 tbsp peanut oil

8 scallions, cut into batons

2 celery stalks, sliced

4½ oz broccoli florets

4½ oz zucchini, sliced

2 garlic cloves, thinly sliced

1 lb baby spinach

rice, to serve

S A U C E

2 cups vegetable stock

2 tbsp light soy sauce

3 tbsp hoisin sauce

½ tsp chili powder

1 tbsp sesame oil

1 Cut the bean curd into 1-inch cubes and set aside until required.

2 Heat the peanut oil in a preheated wok or large skillet.

3 Add the scallions, celery, broccoli, zucchini, garlic, spinach and bean curd to the wok or skillet and stir-fry for 3–4 minutes.

4 To make the sauce, mix together the vegetable stock, soy sauce, hoisin sauce, chili powder and sesame oil in a flameproof casserole and bring to the boil.

5 Add the stir-fried vegetables and bean curd to the saucepan, reduce the heat, cover and simmer for 10 minutes.

6 Transfer the bean curd and vegetables to a warm serving dish and serve with rice.

VARIATION

This recipe has a green vegetable theme, but alter the color and flavor by adding your favorite vegetables.
Add 2¾ oz fresh or canned and drained straw mushrooms with the vegetables in step 2.

Bean Curd with Bell Peppers

Bean curd is perfect for marinating as it readily absorbs flavors for a great tasting main dish.

NUTRITIONAL INFORMATION

Calories ....267 Sugars 2g
Protein ....9g Fat 23g
Carbohydrate ....5g Saturates 3g

   25 MINS   15 MINS

SERVES 4

INGREDIENTS

12 oz bean curd

2 cloves garlic, crushed

4 tbsp soy sauce

1 tbsp sweet chili sauce

6 tbsp sunflower oil

1 onion, sliced

1 green bell pepper, deseeded
   and diced

1 tbsp sesame oil

1 Using a sharp knife, cut the bean curd into bite-sized pieces. Place the bean curd in a shallow non-metallic dish.

2 Mix together the garlic, soy sauce and sweet chili sauce and drizzle over the bean curd. Toss well to coat and leave to marinate for about 20 minutes.

3 Meanwhile, heat the sunflower oil in a large preheated wok.

4 Add the onion to the wok and stir-fry over a high heat until brown and crispy. Remove the onion with a slotted spoon and leave to drain on absorbent paper towels.

5 Add the bean curd to the hot oil and stir-fry for about 5 minutes.

6 Remove all but 1 tablespoon of the sunflower oil from the wok. Add the bell pepper to the wok and stir-fry for 2–3 minutes, or until softened.

7 Return the bean curd and onions to the wok and heat through, stirring occasionally.

8 Drizzle with sesame oil. Transfer to serving plates and serve immediately.

COOK'S TIP

If you are in a real hurry, buy ready-marinated bean curd from your supermarket.

Egg Fried Rice

In this classic Chinese dish, boiled rice is fried with peas, scallions and egg and flavored with soy sauce.

NUTRITIONAL INFORMATION

Calories 203   Sugars 1g
Protein ....9g   Fat 11g
Carbohydrate ...19g   Saturates 2g

🍲 20 MINS   🕐 10 MINS

SERVES 4

INGREDIENTS

⅔ cup long-grain rice

3 eggs, beaten

2 tbsp vegetable oil

2 garlic cloves, crushed

4 scallions, chopped

1 cup cooked peas

1 tbsp light soy sauce

pinch of salt

shredded scallion,
    to garnish

1 Cook the rice in a pan of boiling water for 10-12 minutes, until almost cooked, but not soft. Drain well, rinse under cold water and drain again.

2 Place the beaten eggs in a saucepan and cook over a gentle heat, stirring until softly scrambled.

3 Heat the vegetable oil in a preheated wok or large skillet, swirling the oil around the base of the wok until it is really hot.

4 Add the crushed garlic, scallions and peas and sauté, stirring occasionally, for 1-2 minutes. Stir the rice into the wok, mixing to combine.

5 Add the eggs, light soy sauce and a pinch of salt to the wok or skillet and stir to mix the egg in thoroughly.

6 Transfer the egg fried rice to serving dishes and serve garnished with the shredded scallion.

COOK'S TIP

The rice is rinsed under cold water to wash out the starch and prevent it from sticking together.

Chatuchak Fried Rice

An excellent way to use up leftover rice. Pop it in the freezer as soon as it is cool, and it will be ready to reheat at any time.

NUTRITIONAL INFORMATION

Calories . . . . .241 Sugars 5g
Protein . . . . .7g Fat 5g
Carbohydrate . . .46g Saturates 1g

25 MINS   15 MINS

SERVES 4

INGREDIENTS

1 tbsp sunflower oil

3 shallots, chopped finely

2 garlic cloves, crushed

1 red chili, deseeded and chopped finely

1-inch piece fresh ginger, shredded finely

½ green bell pepper, deseeded and
   sliced finely

2-3 baby eggplants, quartered

90 g/3 oz sugar snap peas or
   snow peas,
   trimmed and blanched

6 baby corn, halved lengthways and
   blanched

1 tomato, cut into 8 pieces

1½ cups bean sprouts

3 cups cooked
   jasmine rice

2 tbsp tomato catsup

2 tbsp light soy sauce

TO GARNISH

fresh cilantro leaves

lime wedges

1   Heat the sunflower oil in a wok or large, heavy skillet over a high heat.

2   Add the shallots, garlic, chili and ginger to the wok or skillet. Stir until the shallots have softened.

3   Add the green bell pepper and baby eggplant and stir well.

4   Add the sugar snap peas or snow peas, baby corn, tomato and bean sprouts. Stir-fry for 3 minutes.

5   Add the cooked jasmine rice to the wok, and lift and stir with two spoons for 4–5 minutes, until no more steam is released.

6   Stir the tomato catsup and soy sauce into the mixture in the wok.

7   Serve the Chatuchak fried rice immediately, garnished with cilantro leaves and lime wedges to squeeze over.

Green-Fried Rice

Spinach is used in this recipe to give the rice a wonderful green coloring. Tossed with the carrot strips, it is a really appealing dish.

NUTRITIONAL INFORMATION

Calories ....139 Sugars 2g
Protein ....3g Fat 7g
Carbohydrate ...18g Saturates 1g

  5 MINS   20 MINS

SERVES 4

INGREDIENTS

⅔ cup long-grain rice

2 tbsp vegetable oil

2 garlic cloves, crushed

1 tsp grated fresh ginger

1 carrot, cut into matchsticks

1 zucchini, diced

8 oz baby spinach

2 tsp light soy sauce

2 tsp light brown sugar

1 Cook the rice in a saucepan of boiling water for about 15 minutes. Drain the rice well, rinse under cold running water and then rinse the rice thoroughly again. Set aside until required.

2 Heat the vegetable oil in a preheated wok or large, heavy-based skillet.

3 Add the crushed garlic and grated fresh ginger to the wok or skillet and stir-fry for about 30 seconds.

4 Add the carrot matchsticks and diced zucchini to the mixture in the wok and stir-fry for about 2 minutes, so the vegetables still retain their crunch.

5 Add the baby spinach and stir-fry for 1 minute, until wilted.

6 Add the rice, soy sauce and sugar to the wok and mix together well.

7 Transfer the green-fried rice to serving dishes and serve immediately.

COOK'S TIP

Light soy sauce has more flavor than the sweeter, dark soy sauce, which gives the food a rich, reddish color.

Vegetable Fried Rice

This dish can be served as part of a substantial meal for a number of people or as a vegetarian meal in itself for four.

NUTRITIONAL INFORMATION

Calories	175	Sugars	.........3g
Protein	.........3g	Fat	..........10g
Carbohydrate	...20g	Saturates	.......2g

10 MINS   20 MINS

SERVES 4

INGREDIENTS

⅔ cup long-grain white rice

3 tbsp peanut oil

2 garlic cloves, crushed

½ tsp Chinese five-spice powder

⅓ cup green beans

1 green bell pepper, seeded and chopped

4 baby corn cobs, sliced

1 oz bamboo shoots, chopped

3 tomatoes, skinned, seeded and chopped

½ cup cooked peas

1 tsp sesame oil

1 Bring a large saucepan of water to the boil.

2 Add the long-grain white rice to the saucepan and cook for about 15 minutes. Drain the rice well, rinse under cold running water and drain thoroughly again.

3 Heat the peanut oil in a preheated wok or large skillet. Add the garlic and Chinese five-spice and stir-fry for 30 seconds.

4 Add the green beans, chopped green bell pepper and sliced corn cobs and stir-fry the ingredients in the wok for 2 minutes.

5 Stir the bamboo shoots, tomatoes, peas and rice into the mixture in the wok and stir-fry for 1 further minute.

6 Sprinkle with sesame oil and transfer to serving dishes. Serve immediately.

VARIATION

Use a selection of vegetables of your choice in this recipe, cutting them to a similar size in order to ensure that they cook in the same amount of time.

Chinese Risotto

Risotto is a creamy Italian dish made with arborio or risotto rice. This Chinese version is simply delicious!

NUTRITIONAL INFORMATION

Calories 436	Sugars 7g
Protein 13g	Fat 14g
Carbohydrate ...70g	Saturates 4g

 5 MINS   25 MINS

SERVES 4

I N G R E D I E N T S

2 tbsp peanut oil

1 onion, sliced

2 cloves garlic, crushed

1 tsp Chinese five-spice powder

8 oz Chinese sausage, sliced

8 oz carrots, diced

1 green bell pepper, deseeded and
  diced

1⅓ cups risotto rice

1¾ cups vegetable or chicken stock

1 tbsp fresh chives

1 Heat the peanut oil in a large preheated wok or heavy-based skillet.

2 Add the onion slices, crushed garlic and Chinese five-spice powder to the wok or skillet and stir-fry for 1 minute.

3 Add the Chinese sausage, carrots and green bell pepper to the wok and stir to combine.

4 Stir in the risotto rice and cook for 1 minute.

5 Gradually add the vegetable or chicken stock, a little at a time, stirring constantly until the liquid has been completely absorbed and the rice grains are tender.

6 Snip the chives with a pair of clean kitchen scissors and stir into the wok with the last of the stock.

7 Transfer the Chinese risotto to warm serving bowls and serve immediately.

COOK'S TIP

Chinese sausage is highly flavored and is made from chopped pork fat, pork meat and spices. Use a spicy Portuguese sausage if Chinese sausage is unavailable.

Chicken Chow Mein

This classic dish requires no introduction as it is already a favorite amongst most Chinese food-eaters.

NUTRITIONAL INFORMATION

Calories	230	Sugars	. . . . .2g
Protein	. . . . .19g	Fat	. . . . .11g
Carbohydrate	. . .14g	Saturates	. . . . . . .2g

5 MINS   20 MINS

SERVES 4

INGREDIENTS

9 oz packet medium egg noodles

2 tbsp sunflower oil

9½ oz cooked chicken breasts, shredded

1 clove garlic, finely chopped

1 red bell pepper, deseeded and thinly sliced

3½ oz shiitake mushrooms, sliced

6 scallions, sliced

1 cup bean sprouts

3 tbsp soy sauce

1 tbsp sesame oil

1 Place the egg noodles in a large bowl or dish and break them up slightly. Pour over enough boiling water to cover the noodles and leave to stand.

2 Heat the sunflower oil in a large preheated wok. Add the shredded chicken, finely chopped garlic, bell pepper slices, mushrooms, scallions and bean sprouts to the wok and stir-fry for about 5 minutes.

3 Drain the noodles thoroughly. Add the noodles to the wok, toss well and stir-fry for a further 5 minutes.

4 Drizzle the soy sauce and sesame oil over the chow mein and toss until well combined.

5 Transfer the chicken chow mein to warm serving bowls and serve immediately.

  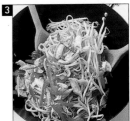

VARIATION

You can make the chow mein with a selection of vegetables for a vegetarian dish, if you prefer.

Cantonese Fried Noodles

This dish is usually served as a snack or light meal. It may also be served as an accompaniment to plain meat and fish dishes.

NUTRITIONAL INFORMATION

Calories	385	Sugars	.........6g
Protein	........38g	Fat	..........17g
Carbohydrate	...21g	Saturates	.......4g

🧊 5 MINS   🕐 15 MINS

SERVES 4

I N G R E D I E N T S

12 oz egg noodles

3 tbsp vegetable oil

1½ lb lean beef steak, cut into thin strips

4½ oz green cabbage, shredded

2¾ oz bamboo shoots

6 scallions, sliced

1 oz green beans, halved

1 tbsp dark soy sauce

2 tbsp beef stock

1 tbsp dry sherry

1 tbsp light brown sugar

2 tbsp chopped parsley, to garnish

1 Cook the noodles in a saucepan of boiling water for 2-3 minutes. Drain well, rinse under cold running water and drain thoroughly again.

2 Heat 1 tablespoon of the oil in a preheated wok or skillet, swirling it around until it is really hot

3 Add the noodles and stir-fry for 1-2 minutes. Drain the noodles and set aside until required.

4 Heat the remaining oil in the wok. Add the beef and stir-fry for 2-3 minutes. Add the cabbage, bamboo shoots, scallions and beans to the wok and stir-fry for 1-2 minutes.

5 Add the soy sauce, beef stock, dry sherry and light brown sugar to the wok, stirring to mix well.

6 Stir the noodles into the mixture in the wok, tossing to mix well. Transfer to serving bowls, garnish with chopped parsley and serve immediately.

VARIATION

You can vary the vegetables in this dish depending on seasonal availability or whatever you have at hand – try broccoli, green bell pepper or spinach.

Lamb with Noodles

Lamb is quick fried, coated in a soy sauce and served on a bed of transparent noodles for a richly flavored dish.

NUTRITIONAL INFORMATION

Calories 285	Sugars 1g
Protein 27g	Fat 16g
Carbohydrate ...10g	Saturates 6g

5 MINS   15 MINS

SERVES 4

INGREDIENTS

5½ oz cellophane noodles

2 tbsp peanut oil

1 lb lean lamb, thinly sliced

2 garlic cloves, crushed

2 leeks, sliced

3 tbsp dark soy sauce

1 cup lamb stock

dash of chili sauce

red chili strips, to garnish

1 Bring a large saucepan of water to the boil. Add the cellophane noodles and cook for 1 minute. Drain the noodles well, place in a sieve, rinse under cold running water and drain thoroughly again. Set aside until required.

2 Heat the peanut oil in a preheated wok or skillet, swirling the oil around until it is really hot.

3 Add the lamb to the wok or skillet and stir-fry for about 2 minutes.

4 Add the crushed garlic and sliced leeks to the wok and stir-fry for a further 2 minutes.

5 Stir in the dark soy sauce, lamb stock and chili sauce and cook for 3-4 minutes, stirring frequently, until the meat

is cooked through.

6 Add the drained cellophane noodles to the wok or skillet and cook for about 1 minute, stirring, until heated through.

7 Transfer the lamb and cellophane noodles to serving plates, garnish with red chili strips and serve.

COOK'S TIP

Transparent noodles are available in Chinese supermarkets. Use egg noodles instead if transparent noodles are unavailable, and cook them according to the instructions on the packet.

Pork Chow Mein

This is a basic recipe – the meat and/or vegetables can be varied as much as you like.

NUTRITIONAL INFORMATION

Calories 239	Sugars 1g	
Protein 17g	Fat 14g	
Carbohydrate ...12g	Saturates 2g	

15 MINS   15 MINS

SERVES 4

I N G R E D I E N T S

9 oz egg noodles

4-5 tbsp vegetable oil

9 oz pork fillet, cooked

4½ oz green beans

2 tbsp light soy sauce

1 tsp salt

½ tsp sugar

1 tbsp Chinese rice wine or dry sherry

2 scallions, finely shredded

a few drops sesame oil

chili sauce, to serve (optional)

1 Cook the noodles in boiling water according to the instructions on the packet, then drain and rinse under cold water. Drain again then toss with 1 tablespoon of the oil.

2 Slice the pork into thin shreds and top and tail the beans.

3 Heat 3 tablespoons of oil in a preheated wok until hot. Add the noodles and stir-fry for 2-3 minutes with 1 tablespoon soy sauce, then remove to a serving dish. Keep warm.

4 Heat the remaining oil and stir-fry the beans and meat for 2 minutes. Add the salt, sugar, wine or sherry, the remaining soy sauce and about half the scallions to the wok.

5 Stir the mixture in the wok, adding a little stock if necessary, then pour on top of the noodles, and sprinkle with sesame oil and the remaining scallions.

6 Serve the chow mein hot or cold with chili sauce, if desired.

COOK'S TIP

Chow Mein literally means 'stir-fried noodles' and is highly popular in the West as well as in China. Almost any ingredient can be added, such as fish, meat, poultry or vegetables. It is very popular for lunch and makes a tasty salad served cold.

Oyster Sauce Noodles

Chicken and noodles are cooked and then tossed in an oyster sauce and egg mixture in this delicious recipe.

NUTRITIONAL INFORMATION

Calories 278	Sugars 2g
Protein 30g	Fat 12g
Carbohydrate ...13g	Saturates 3g

5 MINS   25 MINS

SERVES 4

INGREDIENTS

9 oz egg noodles

1 lb chicken thighs

2 tbsp peanut oil

3½ oz carrots, sliced

3 tbsp oyster sauce

2 eggs

3 tbsp cold water

1 Place the egg noodles in a large bowl or dish. Pour enough boiling water over the noodles to cover and leave to stand for 10 minutes.

2 Meanwhile, remove the skin from the chicken thighs. Cut the chicken flesh into small pieces, using a sharp knife.

VARIATION

Flavor the eggs with soy sauce or hoisin sauce as an alternative to the oyster sauce, if you prefer.

3 Heat the peanut oil in a large preheated wok or skillet, swirling the oil around the base of the wok until it is really hot.

4 Add the pieces of chicken and the carrot slices to the wok and stir-fry for about 5 minutes.

5 Drain the noodles thoroughly. Add the noodles to the wok and stir-fry for a further 2–3 minutes or until the noodles are heated through.

6 Beat together the oyster sauce, eggs and 3 tablespoons of cold water. Drizzle the mixture over the noodles and stir-fry for a further 2–3 minutes or until the eggs set.

7 Transfer the mixture in the wok to warm serving bowls and serve hot.

Noodles with Chili & Shrimp

This is a simple dish to prepare and is packed with flavor, making it an ideal choice for special occasions.

NUTRITIONAL INFORMATION

Calories 259	Sugars 9g
Protein 28g	Fat 8g
Carbohydrate . . .20g	Saturates 1g

 10 MINS   5 MINS

SERVES 4

I N G R E D I E N T S

9 oz thin glass noodles

2 tbsp sunflower oil

1 onion, sliced

2 red chilies, deseeded and very finely chopped

4 lime leaves, thinly shredded

1 tbsp fresh cilantro

2 tbsp palm or superfine sugar

2 tbsp fish sauce

1 lb raw jumbo shrimp, peeled

1 Place the noodles in a large bowl. Pour over enough boiling water to cover the noodles and leave to stand for 5 minutes. Drain thoroughly and set aside until required.

COOK'S TIP

If you cannot buy raw jumbo shrimp, use cooked shrimp instead and cook them with the noodles for 1 minute only, just to heat through.

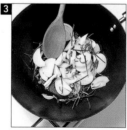

2 Heat the sunflower oil in a large preheated wok or skillet until it is really hot.

3 Add the onion, red chilies and lime leaves to the wok and stir-fry for 1 minute.

4 Add the cilantro, palm or superfine sugar, fish sauce and shrimp to the wok or skillet and stir-fry for a further 2 minutes or until the shrimp turn pink.

5 Add the drained noodles to the wok, toss to mix well, and stir-fry for 1–2 minutes or until heated through.

6 Transfer the noodles and shrimp to warm serving bowls and serve immediately.

Noodles with Shrimp

This is a simple dish using egg noodles and large shrimp, which give the dish a wonderful flavor, texture and color.

NUTRITIONAL INFORMATION

Calories	142	Sugars	.......0.4g
Protein	........11g	Fat	...........7g
Carbohydrate	....11g	Saturates	.......1g

5 MINS 10 MINS

SERVES 4

I N G R E D I E N T S

8 oz thin egg noodles

2 tbsp peanut oil

1 garlic clove, crushed

½ tsp ground star anise

1 bunch scallions, cut into 2-inch pieces

24 raw jumbo shrimp, peeled with tails intact

2 tbsp light soy sauce

2 tsp lime juice

lime wedges, to garnish

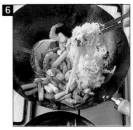

1 Blanch the noodles in a saucepan of boiling water for about 2 minutes.

2 Drain the noodles well, rinse under cold water and drain thoroughly again. Keep warm and set aside until required.

3 Heat the peanut oil in a preheated wok or large skillet until almost smoking.

4 Add the crushed garlic and ground star anise to the wok and stir-fry for 30 seconds.

5 Add the scallions and jumbo shrimp to the wok and stir-fry for 2-3 minutes.

6 Stir in the light soy sauce, lime juice and noodles and mix well.

7 Cook the mixture in the wok for about 1 minute until thoroughly heated through and all the ingredients are thoroughly incorporated.

8 Spoon the noodle and shrimp mixture into a warm serving dish. Transfer to serving bowls, garnish with lime wedges and serve immediately.

COOK'S TIP

If fresh egg noodles are available, these require very little cooking: simply place in boiling water for about 3 minutes, then drain and toss in oil. Noodles can be boiled and eaten plain, or stir-fried with meat and vegetables for a light meal or snack.

Chicken & Noodle One-Pot

Flavorsome chicken and vegetables cooked with Chinese egg noodles in a coconut sauce. Serve in deep soup bowls.

NUTRITIONAL INFORMATION

Calories 256	Sugars 7g
Protein 30g	Fat 8g
Carbohydrate ...18g	Saturates 2g

  5 MINS   20 MINS

SERVES 4

INGREDIENTS

1 tbsp sunflower oil

1 onion, sliced

1 garlic clove, crushed

1 inch fresh ginger, peeled and grated

1 bunch scallions, sliced diagonally

1 lb 2 oz chicken breast fillet, skinned and cut into bite-sized pieces

2 tbsp mild curry paste

2 cups coconut milk

1¼ cups chicken stock

9 oz Chinese egg noodles

2 tsp lime juice

salt and pepper

basil sprigs, to garnish

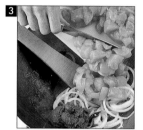

1 Heat the sunflower oil in a wok or large, heavy-based skillet.

2 Add the onion, garlic, ginger and scallions to the wok and stir-fry for 2 minutes until softened.

3 Add the chicken and curry paste and stir-fry for 4 minutes, or until the vegetables and chicken are golden brown. Stir in the coconut milk, stock and salt and pepper to taste, and mix well.

4 Bring to the boil, break the noodles into large pieces, if necessary, add to the pan, cover and simmer for about 6-8 minutes until the noodles are just tender, stirring occasionally.

5 Add the lime juice and adjust the seasoning, if necessary.

6 Serve the chicken and noodle one-pot at once in deep soup bowls, garnished with basil sprigs.

COOK'S TIP

If you enjoy hot flavors, substitute the mild curry paste in the above recipe with hot curry paste but reduce the quantity to 1 tablespoon.

Sweet Fruit Wontons

These sweet wontons are very adaptable and may be filled with whole, small fruits or a spicy chopped mixture as here.

NUTRITIONAL INFORMATION

Calories 244	Sugars 25g
Protein 2g	Fat 12g
Carbohydrate . . .35g	Saturates 3g

10 MINS   15 MINS

SERVES 4

INGREDIENTS

12 wonton wrappers

2 tsp cornstarch

6 tsp cold water

oil, for deep-frying

2 tbsp clear honey

selection of fresh fruit (such as kiwi fruit, limes, oranges, mango and apples), sliced, to serve

FILLING

1 cup chopped dried, pitted dates

2 tsp dark brown sugar

½ tsp ground cinnamon

1 To make the filling, mix together the dates, sugar and cinnamon in a bowl.

2 Spread out the wonton wrappers on a chopping board and spoon a little of the filling into the centre of each wrapper.

COOK'S TIP

Wonton wrappers may be found in Chinese food stores.

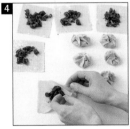

3 Blend the cornstarch and water and brush this mixture around the edges of the wrappers.

4 Fold the wrappers over the filling, bringing the edges together, then bring the two corners together, sealing with the cornstarch mixture.

5 Heat the oil for deep-frying in a wok to 180°C/350°F, or until a cube of bread browns in 30 seconds. Fry the wontons, in batches, for 2–3 minutes, until golden. Remove the wontons from the oil with a slotted spoon and leave to drain on absorbent paper towels.

6 Place the honey in a bowl and stand it in warm water, to soften it slightly. Drizzle the honey over the sweet fruit wontons and serve with a selection of fresh fruit.

Exotic Fruit Salad

This is a sophisticated fruit salad that makes use of some of the exotic fruits that can now be seen in the supermarket.

NUTRITIONAL INFORMATION

Calories 149   Sugars 39g
Protein ....1g   Fat 0.1g
Carbohydrate ...39g   Saturates 0g

10 MINS   15 MINS

SERVES 6

I N G R E D I E N T S

3 granadilla

½ cup superfine sugar

⅔ cup water

1 mango

10 lychees, canned or fresh

1 star-fruit

1 Halve the granadilla and press the flesh through a strainer into a saucepan.

2 Add the sugar and water to the pan and bring to a gentle boil, stirring.

3 Put the mango on a chopping board and cut a thick slice from either side, cutting as near to the pit as possible. Cut away as much flesh as possible in large chunks from the pit section.

COOK'S TIP

A delicious accompaniment to any exotic fruit dish is cardamom cream. Crush the seeds from 8 cardamom pods, add 1¼ cups whipping cream and whip until soft peaks form.

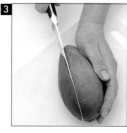 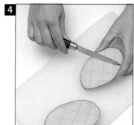 

4 Take the 2 side slices and make 3 cuts through the flesh but not the skin, and 3 more at right angles to make a lattice pattern.

5 Push inside out so that the cubed flesh is exposed and you can easily cut it off.

6 Peel and pit the lychees and cut the star-fruit into 12 slices.

7 Add all the mango flesh, the lychees and star-fruit to the granadilla syrup and poach gently for 5 minutes. Remove the fruit with a perforated spoon.

8 Bring the syrup to the boil and cook for 5 minutes until it thickens slightly.

9 To serve, transfer all the fruit to individual serving glasses, pour over the sugar syrup and serve warm.

Lime Mousse with Mango

Lime-flavored cream molds, served with a fresh mango and lime sauce, make a stunning dessert.

NUTRITIONAL INFORMATION

Calories	254	Sugars	.......17g
Protein	.........5g	Fat	.........19g
Carbohydrate	...17g	Saturates	......12g

10 MINS   0 MINS

SERVES 4

INGREDIENTS

1 cup fromage frais

grated rind of 1 lime

1 tbsp superfine sugar

½ cup heavy cream

MANGO SAUCE

1 mango

juice of 1 lime

4 tsp superfine sugar

TO DECORATE

4 ground cherries

strips of lime rind

1 Put the unsweetened yogurt, lime rind and sugar in a bowl and mix together.

2 Whisk the heavy cream in a separate bowl and fold into the unsweetened yogurt.

3 Line 4 decorative molds or custard pots with cheesecloth or plastic wrap and divide the mixture evenly between them. Fold the cheesecloth over the top and press down firmly.

4 To make the sauce, slice through the mango on each side of the large flat pit, then cut the flesh from the pit. Remove the skin.

5 Cut off 12 thin slices and set aside. Chop the remaining mango, put into a food processor with the lime juice and sugar. Blend until smooth. Alternatively, push the mango through a strainer then mix with the lime juice and sugar.

6 Turn out the molds on to serving plates. Arrange 3 slices of mango on each plate, pour some sauce around, decorate and serve.

COOK'S TIP

Ground Cherries have a tart and mildly scented flavor and make an excellent decoration for many desserts. Peel back the papery husks to expose the bright orange fruits.

This is a Parragon Publishing Book
This edition published in 2001

Parragon Publishing
Queen Street House
4 Queen Street
Bath BA1 1HE, UK

Copyright © Parragon 2000

All rights reserved. No part of this publication may be reproduced, stored in a retrieval system or transmitted,
in any form or by any means, electronic, mechanical, photocopying, recording or otherwise, without the prior
written permission of the copyright holder.

ISBN 0-75254-921-9

Printed in Italy

With grateful thanks to Claire Dashwood.

Material in this book has previously appeared in Ultimate Recipes Low Fat, Ultimate Recipes Vegetarian,
Ultimate Recipes Italian, Ultimate Recipes Chinese, originally produced by Haldane Mason, London.

Notes
Cup measurements in this book are for American cups. Tablespoons are assumed to be 15 ml. Unless
otherwise stated, milk is assumed to be full fat, eggs are medium and pepper is freshly ground black pepper.

The nutritional information provided for each recipe is per serving or per portion. Optional ingredients,
variations or serving suggestions have not been included in the calculations. The times given for each recipe
are an approximate guide only as the preparation times may differ as a result of the type of oven used.